Contents

The Authors

AVERY T. WILLIS JR., the author and developer of *MasterLife*, served as the senior vice-president of overseas operations at the International Mission Board of the Southern Baptist Convention until his retirement in 2004. The original *MasterLife: Discipleship Training for Leaders,* published in 1980, has been used by more than 250,000 people in the United States and has been translated into more than 50 different languages for use by untold thousands. Willis authored many books, including *Indonesian Revival: Why Two Million Came to Christ, The Biblical Basis of Missions, MasterBuilder: Multiplying Leaders, BibleGuide to Discipleship and Doctrine,* and several books in Indonesian.

Willis served for 10 years as a pastor in Oklahoma and Texas and for 14 years as a missionary to Indonesia, during which he served for 6 years as the president of the Indonesian Baptist Theological Seminary. Later he served as the director of the Adult Department of the Discipleship and Family Development Division, the Sunday School Board (now LifeWay Christian Resources) of the Southern Baptist Convention, where he introduced the Lay Institute for Equipping (LIFE), a series of in-depth discipleship courses. Willis went to be with the Lord in 2010.

KAY MOORE served as the coauthor of this updated edition of *MasterLife*. Formerly a design editor in the Adult Department of the Discipleship and Family Development Division, the Sunday School Board of the Southern Baptist Convention, she led the editorial team that produced the LIFE Support Series, biblically based courses that help people deal with critical issues in their lives. A writer, editor, and conference leader, Moore has authored or coauthored numerous books on family life, relationships, and inspirational topics. She is the author of *Gathering the Missing Pieces in an Adopted Life* and is a frequent contributor to religious magazines and devotional guides.

Introduction

MasterLife is a developmental, small-group discipleship process that will help you develop a lifelong, obedient relationship with Christ. This book, *MasterLife 3: The Disciple's Victory,* is the third of four books in that discipleship process. The other three books are *MasterLife 1: The Disciple's Cross*, *MasterLife 2: The Disciple's Personality,* and *MasterLife 4: The Disciple's Mission.* These studies will enable you to acknowledge Christ as your Master and to master life in Him.

WHAT'S IN IT FOR YOU

The goal of *MasterLife* is your discipleship—for you to become like Christ. To do that, you must follow Jesus, learn to do the things He instructed His followers to do, and help others become His disciples. In these ways *MasterLife* will enable you to discover the satisfaction of following Christ as His disciple and the joy of that relationship with Him. *MasterLife* was designed to help you make the following definition of *discipleship* a way of life:

> Christian discipleship is developing a personal, lifelong, obedient relationship with Jesus Christ in which He transforms your character into Christlikeness; changes your values into Kingdom values; and involves you in His mission in the home, the church, and the world.

In *MasterLife 1: The Disciple's Cross* you explored your personal relationship with Jesus Christ. You learned how to draw the Disciple's Cross to illustrate the balanced life Christ wants His disciples to have. You learned that Christ wants to be at the center of your life so that everything you do is an outgrowth of your relationship with Him.

In *MasterLife 2: The Disciple's Personality* you focused on Christ's transforming your character into Christlikeness through the work of the Holy Spirit. You learned how to live a life of victory by building Christlike character. You were introduced to your personal counselor, the Holy Spirit, who lives in you and teaches, guides, directs, prays for, and empowers you to do God's will and work.

This book, *MasterLife 3: The Disciple's Victory,* was designed to help you achieve victory in spiritual warfare. While in book 2 you focused on inner victory, in book 3 you will focus on outer victory as you learn how to advance against the enemy in spiritual warfare. This study also introduces you to the Spiritual Armor. You will learn the defensive weapons of the Spiritual Armor, which protect you, and the offensive weapons, which lead you to advance against the world, the flesh, and the devil. You will learn how to demolish your personal spiritual strongholds and to "take captive every thought to make it obedient to Christ" (2 Cor. 10:5). You will learn to believe God for all He wants to do through you as you practice the six disciplines you learned in *MasterLife 1: The Disciple's Cross:*

- Spend time with the Master
- Live in the Word
- Pray in faith
- Fellowship with believers
- Witness to the world
- Minister to others

THE *MASTERLIFE* PROCESS

MasterLife 3: The Disciple's Victory is part of a 24-week discipleship process. Completing all four courses in *MasterLife* will provide you information and experiences you need to be Christ's disciple. Each book builds on the other and is recommended as a prerequisite for the one that follows.

The *MasterLife* process involves six elements. Each element is essential to your study of *MasterLife.*

1. The *daily activities* in this book lead you into a closer walk with Christ. Doing these exercises daily is important.
2. The *weekly assignments* in "My Walk with the Master This Week" are real-life experiences that will change your life.
3. The *leader* is a major element. Discipleship is a relationship. It is not something you do by yourself. You need human models, instruction, and account-

ability to become what Christ intends for you to be. You need a leader to whom you can relate personally and regularly—someone who can teach you, model behaviors, and hold you accountable.

4. The weekly *group sessions* help you reflect on the concepts and experiences in *MasterLife* and help you apply the ideas to your life. The group sessions allow you to experience the profound changes Christ is making in your life. Each group session also provides training for the next stage of spiritual growth.
5. *Christ* is the Discipler, and you become His disciple. As you fully depend on Him, He works through each of the previous elements to support you.
6. The body of Christ—the *church*—is vital for complete discipling to take place. You depend on Christian friends for fellowship, strength, ministry opportunities, and support.

HOW TO STUDY THIS BOOK

Each day for five days a week you will be expected to study a segment of the material in this workbook and to complete the related activities. You may need from 20 to 30 minutes of study time each day. Even if you find that you can study the material in less time, spreading the study over five days will give you time to apply the truths to your life.

You will notice that discipline logos appear before various assignments. These logos look like this:

These logos link certain activities to the six disciplines you are learning to incorporate into your life as a disciple. These activities are part of your weekly assignments, which are outlined in "My Walk with the Master This Week" at the beginning of each week's material. The discipline logos differentiate your weekly assignments from the activities related to your study for that particular day.

Set a definite time and select a quiet place to study with little or no interruption. Keep a Bible handy to find Scriptures as directed in the material. Memorizing Scripture is an important part of your work. Set aside a portion of your study period for memory work. Unless I have deliberately chosen another version for a specific emphasis, all Scriptures in *MasterLife* are quoted from the *New International Version* of the Bible. However, feel free to memorize Scripture from any version of the Bible you prefer. I suggest that you write each memory verse on a card that you can review often during the week.

After completing each day's assignments, turn to the beginning of the week's material. If you completed an activity that corresponds to one listed under "My Walk with the Master This Week," place a vertical line in the diamond beside the activity. During the following group session a member of the group will verify your work and will add a horizontal line in the diamond, forming a cross in each diamond. This process will confirm that you have completed each weekly assignment before you continue. You may do the assignments at your own pace, but be sure to complete all of them before the next group session.

THE SPIRITUAL ARMOR

On pages 129–31 you will find the Spiritual Armor presentation. The Spiritual Armor, which explains how to use spiritual resources to fight the forces of evil, will be the focal point for all you learn in this book. Each week you will study an additional portion of the Spiritual Armor. By the end of the study you will be able to explain the Spiritual Armor in your own words. As a follower of Christ, you can learn to live the Spiritual Armor so that it embodies how you live in the world.

Discipleship Covenant

To participate in *MasterLife,* you are asked to dedicate yourself to God and to your *MasterLife* group by making the following commitments. You may not currently be able to do everything listed, but by signing this covenant, you pledge to adopt these practices as you progress through the study.

As a disciple of Jesus Christ, I commit myself to—

- acknowledge Jesus Christ as Lord of my life each day;
- attend all group sessions unless providentially hindered;
- spend from 20 to 30 minutes a day as needed to complete all assignments;
- have a daily quiet time;
- keep a Daily Master Communication Guide about the way God speaks to me and I speak to Him;
- be faithful to my church in attendance and stewardship;
- love and encourage each group member;
- share my faith with others;
- keep in confidence anything that others share in the group sessions;
- submit myself to others willingly in accountability;
- become a discipler of others as God gives opportunities;
- support my church financially by practicing biblical giving;
- pray daily for group members.

Judy Campbell 323 330 7671 | Laren Paris (310) 997-8484
Matthew Campbell 323 797 1802 | Angie Colwell (310) 692-5272
Leighton Campbell 310.904.2655 | Sharon Simms-Arenz 2137032490
Christine Maner 310 467 5875
Alvarie Anderson 323-381-0697 323-937-9965

Signed [signature] Date 03/27/22

WEEK 1

Overcoming the Enemy

This Week's Goal

You will be able to describe in your own words the spiritual warfare in which we are engaged and to explain how to apply the Spiritual Armor.

My Walk with the Master This Week

You will complete the following activities to develop the six biblical disciplines. When you have completed each activity, draw a vertical line in the diamond beside it.

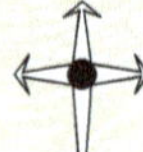

SPEND TIME WITH THE MASTER

◇ Have a quiet time each day. Check each day you have a quiet time: ❑ Sunday ☒ Monday ☒ Tuesday ☒ Wednesday ☒ Thursday ☒ Friday ☒ Saturday

LIVE IN THE WORD

◆ Read your Bible every day. Write what God says to you and what you say to God.

◆ Memorize 1 John 4:4.

◇ Read "How to Read God's Word."

PRAY IN FAITH

◇ Use "Guide to Thanksgiving" during your prayer time.

◇ Use the Spiritual Armor during your prayer time.

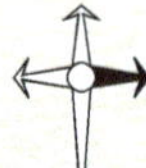

FELLOWSHIP WITH BELIEVERS

◇ Share with someone the Helmet of Salvation part of the Spiritual Armor.

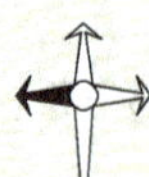

WITNESS TO THE WORLD

◆ List on the Relational-Witnessing Chart the names of persons who do not or may not know Christ. Finish listing your immediate family and relatives.

MINISTER TO OTHERS

◇ Learn the Helmet of Salvation part of the Spiritual Armor.

This Week's Scripture-Memory Verse

"You, dear children, are from God and have overcome them, because the one who is in you is greater than the one who is in the world" (1 John 4:4).

* Genesis 18: 9-33

DAY 1

Under Attack

When our family visited Greece on our way home from our first term of missionary service in Indonesia, I began to understand what Paul had in mind when he wrote 2 Corinthians 10:3-5 (in the margin). I rented a Volkswagen "bug" and crowded our four children into it for a tour of the magnificent ruins of the temples, cities, and amphitheaters of the old Greek civilization.

"Though we live in the world, we do not wage war as the world does. The weapons we fight with are not the weapons of the world. On the contrary, they have divine power to demolish strongholds. We demolish arguments and every pretension that sets itself up against the knowledge of God, and we take captive every thought to make it obedient to Christ" (2 Cor. 10:3-5).

When we reached Corinth, we did not have much time left before we had to return the rental car. Corinth was situated at the base of a huge mountain. We decided that we had enough time to drive to the top, where I had heard that an almost impregnable fortress stood. The little Volkswagen struggled up the mountain until we reached the top. Around the entire top of the mountain was a huge wall wide enough for chariots to drive on. We walked into the fortress to see what was there.

As we went through the first gate, we saw another wall, or fortress, one hundred yards up the mountain. When we reached that one, we saw that farther up the hill was another wall completely encircling the mountain. It was becoming evident why, by the time of Paul, no one had ever been able to defeat the occupants of the fortress. After Paul's death another 1,200 years passed before someone broke through the fortress, and only twice in history did that occur. By the time we reached the third wall, my wife, Shirley, and our two daughters decided to wait for our two boys and me to climb to the top of the mountain.

At the top of the mountain we looked back at Shirley and the girls, who looked about an inch tall. Then I turned around to catch a panoramic view of the Mediterranean Sea. To the left I saw the city of Athens, and if I could have seen far enough to the right, I would have seen the city of Rome. Obviously, whoever held this fortress would have had a very strong position in the ancient world. I realized that the Corinthians to whom Paul wrote would have easily identified with fortresses that needed to be demolished. In light of this description, read again 2 Corinthians 10:3-5 in the margin.

The Corinthians would have easily identified with fortresses that needed to be demolished.

We are in a spiritual battle with the kingdom of darkness. We live behind enemy lines, and we face the forces of Satan. Many fortresses need to be demolished for the kingdom of light to be established.

> A stronghold is an idea, a thought process, a habit, or an addiction through which Satan has set up occupancy in your life—a place where he has the advantage.

This study provides insights into how these spiritual strongholds are established. You will learn how the enemy uses these strongholds to undermine you unless you are armed with the Word and prayer. At the end of this week' study you will be able to—

- define *spiritual warfare*;
- identify the enemy in spiritual warfare;
- describe Jesus' victory over Satan;
- identify three types of spiritual strongholds of evil: personal, ideological, and cosmic;
- practice a plan for demolishing strongholds.

WHAT IS SPIRITUAL WARFARE?

Spiritual warfare is the conflict between the forces of God and the forces of Satan, with the goal being your victory in Christ.

Describe a time when you experienced a conflict like the one described in the definition above.

Negative self Talk - The lies the enemy tells me vs God's truth (Daily)

"That power is like the working of his mighty strength, which he exerted in Christ when he raised him from the dead and seated him at his right hand in the heavenly realms, far above all rule and authority, power and dominion, and every title that can be given, not only in the present age but also in the one to come" (Eph. 1:19-21).

"His intent was that now, through the church, the manifold wisdom of God should be made known to the rulers and authorities in the heavenly realms" (Eph. 3:10).

"Our struggle is not against flesh and blood, but against the rulers, against the authorities, against the powers of this dark world and against the spiritual forces of evil in the heavenly realms" (Eph. 6:12).

Learn what the Bible says about spiritual warfare. In the verses in the margin, underline all references to Satan or spiritual powers.

You probably underlined terms such as "all rule and authority," "rulers and authorities in the heavenly realms," "powers of this dark world," and "spiritual forces of evil in the heavenly realms." The Bible reveals everything God wanted us to know about spiritual warfare.

Check the boxes beside the statements that are true.

- ❑ **Spiritual warfare is no serious threat to me.**
- ❑ **If I read the Bible daily, I will never confront spiritual warfare.**
- ❑ **I try to live a peaceful life. The term *war* does not apply to my lifestyle.**
- ☒ **I live behind enemy lines. Satan's forces can and do attack me.**

Only the last statement is true. Spiritual warfare is a threat to everyone, even the most fervent Christian. Satan will attack anyone—especially those who believe that they are not vulnerable. Therefore, you need to be armed and ready. Strongholds begin in your life when Satan gets a foothold in you. Even if you love peace, Satan would like nothing better than to wage war with you. The moment you start thinking that you are incapable of such behaviors as coveting, raging, or entertaining lustful thoughts, Satan will launch a surprise attack, trying to trip you in the areas you feel most impenetrable. The greater threat you are to him and the kingdom of darkness, the more he attacks you.

THE CONFLICT

We will examine spiritual conflict as Scripture portrays it.

Check the following ways you think Scripture portrays Satan.

☐ **The wicked one**	☐ **The adversary**
☐ **The deceiver**	☐ **The enemy of our souls**
☐ **The destroyer**	☐ **The prince of the power of the air**

All of the previous descriptions of Satan are from Scripture. *Satan* appears as a proper name in the Old Testament, referring to the superhuman enemy of God, humanity, and good (see 1 Chron. 21:1). This word also occurs frequently in the New Testament.

Below are titles the New Testament uses for Satan. Read the Scriptures in the margin and match the references with the titles used.

___ **1. John 12:31**	**a. The tempter**
___ **2. 2 Corinthians 4:4**	**b. The evil one**
___ **3. 1 Thessalonians 3:5**	**c. The prince of this world**
___ **4. Matthew 13:19,38**	**d. The god of this age**
___ **5. Revelation 12:10**	**e. The accuser of our brothers**

Go back and draw a star beside a title that describes an encounter you have had with Satan. Explain why you chose that title.

____

You may have answered something like this: I realize that Satan has been working throughout history to control and destroy, and I am aware of how powerful his influence can be. The answers to the matching exercise are 1. c, 2. d, 3. a, 4. b, 5. e.

SATAN'S CHARACTERISTICS

Satan's power is so great that Michael the archangel viewed him as a foe too powerful to oppose (see Jude 9). The Bible also reveals Satan's influence in worldly events. First John 5:19 declares, "The whole world is under the control of the evil one."

Identify an occurrence in which you believe that Satan was active.

____

Satan is a highly intelligent being. Observe Satan's cunning in tricking Adam and Eve and in taking over their rule of the world:

> *Now the serpent was more crafty than any of the wild animals the Lord God had made. He said to the woman, "Did God really say, 'You must not eat from any tree in the garden'?" The woman said to the serpent, "We may eat fruit from the trees in the garden, but God did say, 'You must not eat fruit from the tree that is in the middle of the garden, and you must not touch it, or you will die.' " "You will not surely die," the serpent said to the woman. "For God knows that when you eat of it your*

"Now is the time for judgment on this world; now the prince of this world will be driven out" (John 12:31).

"The god of this age has blinded the minds of unbelievers, so that they cannot see the light of the gospel of the glory of Christ, who is the image of God" (2 Cor. 4:4).

"For this reason, when I could stand it no longer, I sent to find out about your faith. I was afraid that in some way the tempter might have tempted you and our efforts might have been useless" (1 Thess. 3:5).

"When anyone hears the message about the kingdom and does not understand it, the evil one comes and snatches away what was sown in his heart. This is the seed sown along the path. The field is the world, and the good seed stands for the sons of the kingdom. The weeds are the sons of the evil one" (Matt. 13:19,38).

"The accuser of our brothers, who accuses them before our God day and night, has been hurled down" (Rev. 12:10).

eyes will be opened, and you will be like God, knowing good and evil." (*Gen. 3:1-5*).

Satan also tempted Jesus by offering to give Him all of the kingdoms of the world if Jesus would worship him (see Matt. 4:8-9). He certainly tries to persuade us to sin.

When I think about Satan's power to trick me, I feel—

❑ totally hopeless. How can I attempt to overcome such cunning?
❑ very wary. Satan lies in wait for me at every turn in my life.
☒ confident and sure. With God's power I can have victory over temptation when Satan sets a trap for me.

Sometimes Satan overwhelms you to the point that you feel powerless. God expects you to be wary of the tempter, but He can help you be victorious in spiritual warfare. Look at more of Satan's methods.

Satan uses several means to lead people to sin. Read the verses in the margin and match the references with the means listed below.

C 1. 2 Thessalonians 2:9	**a. Through unforgiveness**
E 2. John 8:44	**b. Through prompting**
D 3. 1 Corinthians 7:5	**c. Through counterfeit miracles, signs, and wonders**
B 4. John 13:2,27	**d. Through your weaknesses**
A 5. 2 Corinthians 2:9-11	**e. Through his lying nature**

Circle the means Satan uses most often to lead you to sin.

Satan's methods are designed to defeat God and humanity by limiting the gospel. He seeks to keep you from giving a verbal testimony and a testimony through example. You will not be able to spread God's Word by your word or by your actions if you give in to Satan, and that is exactly how he tries to silence you. The correct answers are 1. c, 2. e, 3. d, 4. b, 5. a.

Some people do not admit that the enemy exists. But the Bible makes it plain that Satan exists and that his main work is to oppose God's rule in events and in people's lives.

This week's Scripture-memory verse, 1 John 4:4, assures you that you have power over the enemy. To begin your memory work, turn to page 8 and read the verse aloud.

PUTTING ON THE SPIRITUAL ARMOR

Putting on the Spiritual Armor (see Eph. 6:10-20) is a key way you can stand against Satan and his schemes in spiritual warfare. Each week in this study you will learn one part of the Spiritual Armor presentation, which you can find on pages 129–31. By the end of this study you will be able to explain in your own words how to use the Spiritual Armor.

"The coming of the lawless one will be in accordance with the work of Satan displayed in all kinds of counterfeit miracles, signs and wonders" (*2 Thess. 2:9*).

"You belong to your father, the devil, and you want to carry out your father's desire. He was a murderer from the beginning, not holding to the truth, for there is no truth in him. When he lies, he speaks his native language, for he is a liar and the father of lies" (*John 8:44*).

"Do not deprive each other except by mutual consent and for a time, so that you may devote yourselves to prayer. Then come together again so that Satan will not tempt you because of your lack of self-control" (*1 Cor. 7:5*).

"The evening meal was being served, and the devil had already prompted Judas Iscariot, son of Simon, to betray Jesus. As soon as Judas took the bread, Satan entered into him" (*John 13:2,27*).

"The reason I wrote you was to see if you would stand the test and be obedient in everything. If you forgive anyone, I also forgive him. And what I have forgiven—if there was anything to forgive—I have forgiven in the sight of Christ for your sake, in order that Satan might not outwit us. For we are not unaware of his schemes" (*2 Cor. 2:9-11*).

Begin learning the Spiritual Armor presentation today by studying the Helmet of Salvation. Turn to page 129 and read the entire presentation, with special emphasis on the Helmet of Salvation.

The Helmet of Salvation should remind you to—

1. thank God that you are His child;
2. praise God for your eternal life;
3. claim the mind of Christ.

Focusing on the first instruction, stop and thank God that you are His child. Thank Him for your salvation.

The guide that follows will help you give thanks to God. Read it and use it in your prayer time.

GUIDE TO THANKSGIVING

Thanksgiving lays the foundation for other forms of prayer. Use these guidelines to make thanksgiving a part of every prayer.

1. The source of thanksgiving is grace. Thanks is our reaction when we realize that all we have, receive, and are is a gift of God's grace. Thanksgiving is rejoicing at what God gave when we were undeserving. True gratitude registers surprise that God could be so good to us when we deserve nothing. (See Acts 27:35; 28:15; Rom. 6:17; 1 Cor. 1:4; Col. 1:12; Rev. 11:17.)
2. The condition of thanksgiving is agreement. Thanksgiving means that you agree with God. Thus, the Bible encourages you to give thanks in all circumstances (see 1 Thess. 5:18) and to pray about the things that concern you most by making your petitions with thanksgiving (see Phil. 4:6).
3. The response of thanksgiving is worship. Thanksgiving responds to God's specific acts. Praise and thanks are thus natural partners in worship (see Ps. 100:4; Heb. 13:15). Your prayers and your actions worship your Creator. When you thank God, you enter His presence, worship Him, and present an offering to Him.
4. The occasion for thanksgiving is everything. Nothing should escape your thanksgiving. God is active in every area of your life and can show you His direction even in the darkest hour. Thanking God frees Him to work in your life through those circumstances.
5. The reward of thanksgiving is the enjoyment of God's blessings: peace, joy, growth, worship, and life in Christ. If you have trouble giving thanks under any circumstance, ask the Spirit to fill you (see Eph. 5:18-20).

Read Psalm 119:1-8 during your quiet time today. Let God speak to you through this passage. Then complete the Daily Master Communication Guide in the margin.

DAILY MASTER COMMUNICATION GUIDE

PSALM 119:1-8

What God said to me:

You will be blessed when you are obedient and follow me; follow my ways and my commands.

What I said to God:

God I will be obedient and follow you, your ways and your commands. I am sorry for the times that I have been disobedient and I pray that you forgive me. Thank you.

You, dear children are from God and overcome them, because the one who is in you is greater than the one who is in the world.
1 John 4:4

DAY 2

Defining the Battleground

As you learned in day 1, the devil is strong. However, through the Lord, Christians are stronger than the devil. They have the protection they need to withstand Satan's assaults. Satan tempts, but God provides a way of escape, as 1 Corinthians 10:13, in the margin, states.

"No temptation has seized you except what is common to man. And God is faithful; he will not let you be tempted beyond what you can bear. But when you are tempted, he will also provide a way out so that you can stand up under it" (1 Cor. 10:13).

Many times when I have been tempted, the Holy Spirit has brought to mind a verse I had memorized. Then I began to look for the way to escape the temptation.

SPIRITUAL BATTLE

We can triumph because Jesus triumphed over Satan and his forces in His death and resurrection. Read Colossians 2:15 in the margin.

"Having disarmed the powers and authorities, he made a public spectacle of them, triumphing over them by the cross" (Col. 2:15).

How did Jesus triumph over Satan? Circle all that apply.

incarnation  **crucifixion**  **resurrection**

In His crucifixion and resurrection Christ triumphed over the devil. Of course, He had to come in the incarnation to fight the battle as a human being. This week's Scripture-memory verse assures you of that victory.

Stop and begin hiding in your heart this week's Scripture-memory verse, 1 John 4:4. Write it in the margin from one to three times.

The battle is spiritual in nature, and your weapons are spiritual, not weapons of the world.

"Though we live in the world, we do not wage war as the world does. The weapons we fight with are not the weapons of the world. On the contrary, they have divine power to demolish strongholds. We demolish arguments and every pretension that sets itself up against the knowledge of God, and we take captive every thought to make it obedient to Christ" (2 Cor. 10:3-5).

In the margin read the verses from 2 Corinthians that you read at the beginning of this week's work. Underline what kind of power is possessed by the weapons you use in spiritual battle.

The weapons we use in spiritual battle have the divine power to demolish strongholds. These verses promise you that you have the power to take all thoughts captive and to make them obedient to Christ.

This week you will study three types of spiritual strongholds that define the battleground for spiritual warfare:

- Personal strongholds
- Ideological strongholds
- Cosmic strongholds

Today you will study the first type of stronghold.

PERSONAL STRONGHOLDS

Christians struggle against the world, the flesh, and the devil. In *MasterLife 2: The Disciple's Personality* the term *flesh* was used to define the body and the sinful nature. In this study I will use a broader definition of it. Watchman Nee defines *flesh* as "any attitude or action done without total dependence on the Lord Jesus Christ."[1]

Personal strongholds are areas of our lives in which we are most vulnerable to Satan's attacks. They are areas in which Satan always seems to get advantage of you.

Satan first attacks the flesh, which is the inner tendency and capacity to sin. Through the flesh Satan influences the mind, the will, and the emotions. He wants us to depend on ourselves and on our own strength. Paul warns you "not to give the devil a foothold" (Eph. 4:27). Satan's footholds soon become his strongholds if not defeated by spiritual weapons.

Satan's footholds soon become his strongholds if not defeated by spiritual weapons.

Check all that apply:

- ❑ **I have no spiritual strongholds.**
- ❑ **I have one or more spiritual strongholds.**
- ☒ **Satan may have a foothold in one or more areas of my life.**

If part of your life is not fully committed to God, name that area and describe ways it is vulnerable to satanic attack.

My Dreams / professional life - satan can use discouragement / rejection to attack my faith.

In the Sermon on the Mount Jesus taught how to deal with several basic areas that can become personal strongholds of Satan:

☒ **bitterness**	❑ **religious ritual**
❑ **lust**	☒ **greed**
☒ **improper speech**	❑ **pride**

In the previous list, check the strongholds in your life. In the margin add others you discovered through the "In the Carpenter's Shop" sections of *MasterLife 2: The Disciple's Personality.*

DEMOLISHING PERSONAL SPIRITUAL STRONGHOLDS

During this study you will identify ways the Holy Spirit is helping you build Christlike character as you select strongholds to be demolished and character traits to be built up in Christlikeness. This is the next step in the process of Christian character building you began in book 2.

Read the verses in the margin, which deal with the stronghold of bitterness. Then describe the area of bitterness in your life that needs to be demolished, what you need to do to demolish it, and the

"You have heard that it was said, 'Eye for eye, and tooth for tooth.' But I tell you, Do not resist an evil person. If someone strikes you on the right cheek, turn to him the other also. And if someone wants to sue you and take your tunic, let him have your cloak as well. If someone forces you to go one mile, go with him two miles. Give to the one who asks you, and do not turn away from the one who wants to borrow from you. You have heard that it was said, 'Love your neighbor and hate your enemy.' But I tell you: Love your enemies and pray for those who persecute you, that you may be sons of your Father in heaven. He causes his sun to rise on the evil and the good, and sends rain on the righteous and the unrighteous" (Matt. 5:38-45).

Bitterness towards my family
" " " supervisor

DAILY MASTER COMMUNICATION GUIDE

PSALM 119:9-16

What God said to me:

You can stay pure, by living according to my word. I will not let you stray from my commands if you seek me with all your heart. Hide my word in your heart, that you might not sin against me.

What I said to God:

God I want to live according to your word, Please help me to do so. God I believe that you will cover me and I believe your promises to me. I will hide your word in my heart so I will not sin against you and know what you desire of me.

spiritual weapon(s) to be used in demolishing it. Later this week you will record your progress. Here is an example.

Stronghold to be demolished: bitterness toward my boss

What I need to do to demolish it: pray for my boss instead of harboring anger toward him

Spiritual weapons to be used: Helmet of Salvation—claim the mind of Christ; Sword of the Spirit—learn what God's Word says about bitterness and its results

Now you try it.

Stronghold to be demolished: Bitterness toward my supervisor

What I need to do to demolish it: pray for my supervisor instead of harboring anger towards her

Spiritual weapon(s) to be used: Helmet of salvation - claim the mind of Christ, sword of the Spirit - learn what God's word says about bitterness and its results.

When you demolish a stronghold, this does not mean that you will never again be tempted in this area, but it does mean that Satan will not set up camp inside you to entrap you in his snares.

Read Psalm 119:9-16 during your quiet time today. Then complete the Daily Master Communication Guide in the margin.

DAY 3

Outside Influences

This week you are studying three types of spiritual strongholds that define the battleground for spiritual warfare:

- Personal strongholds
- Ideological strongholds
- Cosmic strongholds

Today you will study the second type of spiritual stronghold.

IDEALOGICAL STRONGHOLDS

Idealogical strongholds are built around systems of thought and ideas that are embodied in cultures and that exert pressure on members of that culture. Through this influence, which the Bible calls the world, a whole society begins to hold certain values. What Satan does to individuals through the flesh, he does to society through the world. Over time personal strongholds become embodied in cultures as strongholds.

In the world you find "arguments and every pretension that sets itself up against the knowledge of God" (2 Cor. 10:5). The world includes the following.

❑ **philosophical systems**	☒ **educational systems**
☒ **value systems**	☒ **religious systems**
☒ **economic systems**	❑ **political systems**

In the previous list check the systems you have seen or experienced Satan using as a stronghold.

Systems Satan has used could include Communism; capitalism, when it leads people to turn their backs on the poor; humanism; Darwinism; and dictatorships. They can also include claims of intolerance. If you say that you are a Christian, some people automatically respond that you are a bigot. Christians encounter claims that they are intolerant when they take stands against such issues as homosexuality, abortion, and pornography. These claims subtly destroy our society's sense of right and wrong.

Strongholds of Satan could also include—

- the gambling industry;
- pornography in the name of freedom of speech;
- the sexual revolution;
- secularism;
- the religious revolution in America, which has embraced other world religions and has created new ones.

Were you surprised to see religious systems on the list? I am talking about the hollow, ritualistic religion the Pharisees exhibited in which the focus becomes an addictive effort to do the right thing rather than a dependent, personal relationship with God. Jesus said that the Pharisees and their religious system were from their father, the devil. Paul warned, "See to it that no one takes you captive through hollow and deceptive philosophy, which depends on human tradition and the basic principles of this world rather than on Christ" (Col. 2:8).

Read 1 Corinthians 10:13 in the margin. Underline the phrase that tells what God does when you are tempted.

"No temptation has seized you except what is common to man. And God is faithful; he will not let you be tempted beyond what you can bear. But when you are tempted, he will also provide a way out so that you can stand up under it" (1 Cor. 10:13).

"Everyone born of God overcomes the world. This is the victory that has overcome the world, even our faith" (1 John 5:4).

"I urge you, brothers, in view of God's mercy, to offer your bodies as living sacrifices, holy and pleasing to God—this is your spiritual act of worship. Do not conform any longer to the pattern of this world, but be transformed by the renewing of your mind. Then you will be able to test and approve what God's will is—his good, pleasing and perfect will" (Rom. 12:1-2).

Daily Master Communication Guide

Psalm 119:17-24

What God said to me:

Open your eyes so that you may see the things that I want you to see concerning me. Follow my commandments (commands) and that will be your guide to what you need to do.

What I said to God:

God please open my eyes. I want to see things of you O God. Help me to see what you want me to see. Please help me O God to follow your commands and that which you call me to do. Please help me to be obedient to your word.

Read 1 John 5:4 in the margin on page 17. Write the word that identifies how you have victory to overcome the world.

Salvation

The flesh and the world are the devil's habitats, but that does not mean spirit possession. In the Bible, people possessed by evil spirits were not yet Christians. Because you are a Christian, God has given you the power to escape any temptation. Your faith is the victory that claims God's power over the world, the flesh, and the devil.

Based on this week's Scripture-memory verse, what do you have that is greater than the tempter in the world?

Christ in me

Christ, who lives in you, gives you the victory over the world and its tempter, Satan.

Romans 12:1-2, in the margin on page 17, gives Christians an antidote to the world's systems.

PUTTING ON THE SPIRITUAL ARMOR

As you think about fighting the evil systems of the world, recall the weapons you are learning in the Spiritual Armor presentation.

Stop and pray through each weapon below, as shown in the Spiritual Armor presentation on pages 129–31.

- **Helmet of Salvation** Eph 6:17
- **Breastplate of Righteousness** Eph 6:14
- **Belt of Truth** Eph 6:14
- **Gospel Shoes** Eph 6:15
- **Shield of Faith** Eph 6:16
- **Sword of the Spirit** Eph 6:17

In day 1 you learned three instructions to follow in putting on the Helmet of Salvation. Review them on page 13.

Take the second step in putting on the Helmet of Salvation by praising God for eternal life. Stop and praise God for the security of eternal life you have in Jesus Christ.

Read Psalm 119:17-24 during your quiet time today. Let God speak to you through this passage. Then complete the Daily Master Communication Guide in the margin.

DAY 4

To Steal, Kill, and Destroy

Satan rules a group of evil spirits that, with the aid of humanity, establishes a counterculture of sin defying God's righteous order. Its goal is to oppose God's work and to steal, kill, and destroy.

This week you are studying three types of spiritual strongholds that define the battleground for spiritual warfare:

- Personal strongholds
- Ideological strongholds
- Cosmic strongholds.

Today you will examine the third stronghold, which centers on the satanic counterculture.

COSMIC STRONGHOLDS

Read the verses from John 10 in the margin. Then answer the following.

"I tell you the truth, the man who does not enter the sheep pen by the gate, but climbs in by some other way, is a thief and a robber. The man who enters by the gate is the shepherd of his sheep. The thief comes only to steal and kill and destroy; I have come that they may have life, and have it to the full" (John 10:1-2,10).

What does Jesus, the Good Shepherd, offer? Life to the full

What is Satan's purpose? Steal, kill, and destroy

What is the way to life at its fullest? Entering through the gate. (Jesus)

Jesus Christ is the only way to salvation. The world offers many alluring ways that appear to provide enjoyment and pleasure, but the world's promises are shallow. People who believe Satan's lies find themselves on a path of destruction that leads away from the abundant life in Jesus.

In the world around us—in the atmosphere—are evil beings under Satan's leadership. When I was in seminary, some scholars claimed that evil spirits were psychological states of mind. The devil was dismissed as a general force or thought that represented evil, natural forces in humankind. At the same time, I met missionaries who were encountering many manifestations of Satan and his evil spirits in other cultures. When I went abroad as a missionary, I did not claim that the evil spirits did not exist. Instead, I emphasized that the Holy Spirit of God, through the victory of Jesus Christ, is more powerful than any evil spirit or satanic representative (see Col. 2:13-15 in the margin).

"When you were dead in your sins and in the uncircumcision of your sinful nature, God made you alive with Christ. He forgave us all our sins, having canceled the written code, with its regulations, that was against us and that stood opposed to us; he took it away, nailing it to the cross. And having disarmed the powers and authorities, he made a public spectacle of them, triumphing over them by the cross" (Col. 2:13-15).

In recent years Satan's forces have gained so many strongholds in the United States that Americans have begun to be aware of evil spirits, the occult, mediums, channeling, demon possession, and satanic worship. Obviously, all of these are not merely psychological interpretations: "Our struggle is not against flesh and blood, but against the rulers, against the authorities, against the powers of this dark world and against the spiritual forces of evil in the heavenly realms" (Eph. 6:12). Strongholds in the heavenlies, or the atmosphere around us, seem to be the abodes of various kinds of spiritual beings that fight against the cause of God and Christ. In the Old Testament the prince of Persia prevented the angel from coming to Daniel until the archangel Michael helped him. Read Daniel 10:13 in the margin.

"The prince of the Persian kingdom resisted me twenty-one days. Then Michael, one of the chief princes, came to help me, because I was detained there with the king of Persia" (Dan. 10:13).

Some people use the term *strategic spiritual warfare* to refer to the aggressive confrontation of Satan and his demons by intercessors. In the wilderness, in the garden of Gethsemane, and at other critical times in His ministry Jesus showed us how to confront Satan. A word of caution, however: many present-day teachings seem to be based more on experience than on biblical teaching. Bring your experiences in line with the Bible and avoid interpreting the Bible to fit your experiences.

Christ has already won the victory over spiritual forces of evil. We need to claim it and exalt Christ. He will lead in victory.

Bring your experiences in line with the Bible and avoid interpreting the Bible to fit your experiences.

ALERT TO THE ENEMY

Christians need to be alert to the reality of spiritual warfare. In the following list check any positive results you may have already experienced from being more attuned to spiritual warfare.

An awareness of spiritual warfare—

- ☒ **makes Christians more aware of Satan and his forces;**
- ☒ **helps Christians realize that they are in a cosmic spiritual battle;**
- ☒ **prompts Christians to study the Scriptures to understand Satan's deceptions, temptations, persecutions, and occult practices;**
- ☒ **helps identify major schemes of the devil, which include unforgiveness, accusations, distractions, deception, manipulation, division, confusion, discouragement, despair, and heresy;**
- ☒ **helps Christians learn to depend on God for victory.**

Check any of the following consequences of dwelling unduly on spiritual warfare that you have experienced or seen.

An overemphasis on spiritual warfare—

- ☒ **causes people to become preoccupied with Satan and his forces instead of with God. Undue attention to satanic forces may make people more vulnerable to them.**
- ☒ **causes people to attribute to Satan actions that result from the flesh and the world. We should take responsibility for our sins instead of saying, "The devil made me do it."**

- ☐ causes people to put undue emphasis on directly rebuking Satan. Not even Michael the archangel dared to do that (see Jude 9). Some practices of rebuking Satan sound as if the person is praying to the devil instead of to God.
- ☐ causes people to put undue emphasis on directly binding Satan. Jesus is the one who binds the strong man, as Matthew 12:28-29, in the margin, states.

"If I drive out demons by the Spirit of God, then the kingdom of God has come upon you. Or again, how can anyone enter a strong man's house and carry off his possessions unless he first ties up the strong man? Then he can rob his house" (Matt. 12:28-29).

What does this week's Scripture-memory verse, 1 John 4:4, say about Satan's power in comparison to God's power? Practice your memory work by saying this verse aloud to someone today.

Stop and pray that you will keep a proper perspective on your attitude about spiritual warfare while always being aware of your need to claim Christ's victory over the enemy.

PUTTING ON THE SPIRITUAL ARMOR

As you are learning, the Spiritual Armor is a useful means of dealing with spiritual battles. Review on page 13 the three instructions for putting on the Helmet of Salvation.

Practice the third instruction by claiming the mind of Christ. First Corinthians 2:16 says,

"Who has known the mind of the Lord
that he may instruct him?"
But we have the mind of Christ.

The mind of Christ was given to you with your salvation. Stop now and thank God that you have the mind of Christ as you experience spiritual struggles and victories.

The mind of Christ was given to you with your salvation.

Explain to your family, a Christian friend, or a group the Helmet of Salvation part of the Spiritual Armor. God will help you find a way to minister to the person(s).

Use the Spiritual Armor in your prayer life this week.

DEMOLISHING PERSONAL SPIRITUAL STRONGHOLDS

In day 2 you identified a stronghold you wanted to demolish in the area of bitterness or a wrong attitude or action. Give a progress report on how you are using the spiritual weapon(s) you listed to demolish this stronghold.

How I am using a spiritual weapon(s) to help demolish bitterness:

Daily Master Communication Guide

Psalm 119:25-32

What God said to me:

those who trust in Me will not be put to Shame. Don't allow the weight of the world to boggle you down, Put your trust in Me and allow Me to Carry you through.

What I said to God:

Please God, Help me to put me to put all of my trust in you. teach me o Lord, how to give everything over to you so that I will not be weighed down by the things of this world. Amen.!

I am spending more time in the word of God so I am more aware of the attack on my mind, so I can stop them in their tracks.

RELATIONAL WITNESSING

No doubt your heightened awareness about Satan's attacks and humans' vulnerability to them has made you aware of persons who do not know Christ. Perhaps you realize their need to know Him so that they will have His power in their lives. If you have not already done so, begin consciously to let Christ flow through your personal relationships. Three basic types of personal witnessing can be used:

1. *Relational witnessing*—sharing Christ through kinship and friendship
2. *Lifestyle witnessing*—sharing Christ with persons you meet in the normal traffic pattern of your life
3. *Visitation witnessing*—intentionally visiting someone to share Christ

Begin where you are to reach persons for Christ in your circles of influence. This simple procedure can progress as slowly or as quickly as you desire:

1. List on the Relational-Witnessing Chart (p. 135) and on the Prayer-Covenant List (p. 143) family members and relatives who you think may not know Christ. In the following weeks you will list persons in each circle of influence in your life.
2. Evaluate your relationship with each person. We often hesitate to witness to our relatives because our lives have not been as they should be. Now that you have studied two *MasterLife* books, the testimony of your life should be improving.
3. Regularly pray for these persons. Enlist others to pray for them. Prayer plows the soil of the heart for the seed of the gospel to be planted later.
4. Serve them by discovering and meeting their needs. When you serve others because of your love for them and because you are Christ's servant, the Holy Spirit will work in their hearts.
5. Relate Christ's provision to their needs. As you pray, open lines of communication, and serve them, the Holy Spirit will provide opportunities to witness.

Begin to list persons for each circle of influence on the Relational-Witnessing Chart (p. 135) who do not or may not know Christ. Also write their names on the Prayer-Covenant List on page 143. Finish the list for your immediate family and relatives.

Read Psalm 119:25-32 during your quiet time today. Let God speak to you through this passage. Then complete the Daily Master Communication Guide in the margin.

DAY 5

Winning the Victory

All Christians engage in spiritual warfare on personal, ideological, and cosmic levels as they confront the world, the flesh, and the devil. Christ has won the victory over all evil powers and gives victory to Christians who totally depend on Him and use the spiritual weapons He gives. We face an escalation of spiritual warfare and must use God's power to overcome Satan and his forces. First Peter 5:8-9, in the margin, confirms the fact that the devil is alive and well and is waiting to attack.

"Be self-controlled and alert. Your enemy the devil prowls around like a roaring lion looking for someone to devour. Resist him, standing firm in the faith, because you know that your brothers throughout the world are undergoing the same kind of sufferings" (1 Pet. 5:8-9).

Those who wrestle with personal strongholds also need to fight the ideological systems of the world so that we can live holy lives and fulfill God's mission for us in the world. Let's look further at 2 Corinthians 10:3-5, which began our study and which addresses the matter of Satan's attack. Read those verses in the margin.

SPIRITUAL WEAPONS

The Greek word for *weapons* is *panoplia* (from which the English word *panoply* is derived). The *panoplia* was the complete equipment used by the Greeks' heavily armed infantry. Weapons, then, refers to the complete array of spiritual helps God supplies for overcoming the devil's temptations.

List weapons the world uses to fight.

Guns, Knives, Fist, Feet
___

You may have listed tangible weapons like fists, guns, knives, and other objects that cause physical harm. You may have also listed intangible weapons like slander, gossip, and backbiting. Second Corinthians 10:3-5 clearly indicates that Christians are to choose other ways to fight besides these harmful choices.

"Though we live in the world, we do not wage war as the world does. The weapons we fight with are not the weapons of the world. On the contrary, they have divine power to demolish strongholds. We demolish arguments and every pretension that sets itself up against the knowledge of God, and we take captive every thought to make it obedient to Christ" (2 Cor. 10:3-5).

Logic, physical efforts, positive thinking, and psychological tactics will not win over Satan. Only the spiritual weapons God gives you can win spiritual victories.

Read Ephesians 6:11-18 in the margin on the next page. Underline the six weapons God supplies for the battle against Satan.

Another significant word in 2 Corinthians 10:3-5 is *demolish*, which comes from a Greek word meaning *a taking down* or *a pulling down*. You are in the process of pulling down strongholds of the devil, like a demolition crew tearing down an old building by using a wrecking ball.

"Put on the full armor of God so that you can take your stand against the devil's schemes. For our struggle is not against flesh and blood, but against the rulers, against the authorities, against the power of this dark world and against the spiritual forces of evil in the heavenly realms. Therefore put on the full armor of God, so that when the day of evil comes, you may be able to stand your ground, and after you have done everything, to stand. Stand firm then, with the belt of truth buckled around your waist, with the breastplate of righteousness in place, and with your feet fitted with the readiness that comes from the gospel of peace. In addition to all this, take up the shield of faith, with which you can extinguish all the flaming arrows of the evil one. Take the helmet of salvation and the sword of the Spirit, which is the word of God. And pray in the Spirit on all occasions with all kinds of prayers and requests. With this in mind, be alert and always keep on praying for all the saints" (Eph. 6:11-18).

DEMOLISHING PERSONAL SPIRITUAL STRONGHOLDS

In day 2 you identified a stronghold you wanted to demolish in the area of bitterness. Give a progress report on how well you have used the spiritual weapon(s) you listed to demolish this stronghold.

How I have used a spiritual weapon(s) to help demolish bitterness:

Sword of the spirit - to remind myself who I am in God.

Demolishing strongholds is not easy. You will encounter claims that threaten to undermine your faith, and you will have thoughts that do not honor Christ.

As you have studied this week, you may have been frightened by teachings about the enemy. Do not let Satan frighten you. Christ has defeated this foe. Jesus said that He came to give you abundant life in opposition to the one who steals, kills, and destroys. Over the next weeks you will be equipped through the Spiritual Armor to stand victorious and, when the battle is over, to be left standing. Remember that you are studying the disciple's victory, not just spiritual warfare.

HOW TO DEMOLISH A STRONGHOLD

Here is a brief summary of how to demolish a stronghold. You may photocopy this summary and keep it in your Bible, wallet, or another convenient place for ready reference when you need it.

1. Identify the wrong argument or pretension that establishes itself against God. Identify what is wrong with it.
2. Identify the ways the stronghold has become established—through the flesh, desire, society, or the devil. Read 1 John 4:1-6 about testing the spirits.
3. Identify the spiritual weapons for the warfare, in contrast to the worldly solutions.
4. Declare war on the thought or pretension that positions itself against the knowledge of Christ by—
   a. using thoughts or arguments from the Word;
   b. claiming the mind of Christ;
   c. using spiritual weapons (see Eph. 6:11-17), followed by asking for the power of the Spirit through prayer (see Eph. 6:18);
   d. boldly making the truth of the gospel clear (see Eph. 6:19);
   e. claiming the victory by faith.
      - Remember, "the one who is in you is greater than the one who is in the world" (1 John 4:4).
      - Christ has defeated Satan and has spoiled all of the principalities.

5. Win the victory promised in 1 John 5:2-3,18-20 (read these verses in the margin) by—
   a. loving God (see 1 John 5:3);
   b. keeping His commandments (see 1 John 5:3);
   c. being sure that you are born of God;
   d. believing that Jesus is God's Son;
   e. believing that because God keeps you safe, the evil one cannot harm you (see 1 John 5:18).

"This is how we know that we love the children of God: by loving God and carrying out his commands. This is love for God: to obey his commands. And his commands are not burdensome. We know that anyone born of God does not continue to sin; the one who was born of God keeps him safe, and the evil one cannot harm him. We know that we are children of God, and that the whole world is under the control of the evil one. We know also that the Son of God has come and has given us understanding, so that we may know him who is true. And we are in him who is true—even in his Son Jesus Christ. He is the true God and eternal life" (1 John 5:2-3,18-20).

Read John 15:5 in the margin. What does this verse say about spiritual warfare?

"I am the vine; you are the branches. If a man remains in me and I in him, he will bear much fruit; apart from me you can do nothing" (John 15:5).

One should remain in christ because He is the center of their life and without Him they can do nothing

You may have answered: All my thinking should reflect the fact that Christ is the center of my life. Without Him I can do nothing, including evaluating the thoughts and claims that come from the world.

While the world might use weapons like the ones you listed on page 23, a follower of Christ uses the Sword of the Spirit—God's Word—to wage war. You will use this weapon in the following three activities.

By now you have likely memorized this week's Scripture-memory verse, 1 John 4:4. Say it to a family member or a friend.

Read Psalm 119:33-40 during your quiet time today. Let God speak to you. Then complete the Daily Master Communication Guide in the margin on page 26.

Learn to handle the Sword of the Spirit effectively. The following material will help you get more from your Bible reading and study.

HOW TO READ GOD'S WORD

Listen to God speak as you read His Word.

1. Read the Bible systematically. Read through an entire book of the Bible, more or less a chapter a day. Balance your choice of books by reading different types of writings in the Bible.
2. Listen to God speak in one of the four areas for which the Bible states it is to be used: teaching—teaching the faith, rebuking—correcting error, correcting—resetting the direction of a person's life, and training—training a person in right living (see 2 Tim. 3:16-17). As you read the Bible, review these four areas until you automatically recognize when God is speaking in these ways.

Daily Master Communication Guide

Psalm 119:33-40

What God said to me:

Do not focus on the things of the world and selfish things, but focus on knowing me and the things I desire of you and you will have all that you need.

What I said to God:

God please help me to keep my eyes focused on you and your commands. Please help me to not get so caught up in things of the world, but to love and do things concerning you God.

3. Mark words, phrases, and verses that appeal to you. In the margin you may want to place *M* beside verses you want to memorize, *T* beside verses with significant teachings for your life, *C* for correcting life's course, *R* for rebuke, or *I* for instruction in right living. Periodically review verses you have marked in a category.
4. Summarize what God has said to you through the Scripture. You may want to use *Day by Day in God's Kingdom: A Discipleship Journal.* This journal not only suggests Scriptures and memory verses but also provides room for you to record what you experience in your quiet time.[2] Review what you record. See whether a pattern emerges.
5. Pray about what God has said to you. Use the Daily Master Communication Guide format to write what God says to you and what you say to God. If you use this plan regularly, it will become second nature to you as you talk with God. Later, as you review your notes, you will see patterns in what God has communicated to you over a period of time.
6. Be persistent until you are consistent. Aim for consistency rather than for length of time spent.

HAS THIS WEEK MADE A DIFFERENCE?

Review "My Walk with the Master This Week" at the beginning of this week's material. Mark the activities you have finished by drawing vertical lines in the diamonds beside them. Finish any incomplete activities. Think about what you will say during your group session about your work on these activities.

As you complete your study of "Overcoming the Enemy," read the following statements and check all that apply.

- ☒ **I am more aware than ever of how Satan tries to overpower me.**
- ☒ **I am committed to using God's Word and prayer as weapons against Satan's attacks.**
- ☒ **I am trying to replace Satan's strongholds in my life with Christlike character traits.**
- ☒ **I truly desire to make Christ the center of my life by taking each thought captive and evaluating it against Christ's standard.**

Acknowledging that Satan has a grasp on an area of your life takes courage. Being aware that you are vulnerable is a healthy first step to loosening Satan's grip and to replacing his ways with Christlike ways. As you continue this study, you will be armed with more weapons to use in this spiritual battle.

---

1. Edward Rommen, ed., *Spiritual Power and Missions: Raising the Issues* (Pasadena, CA: William Carey Library, 1995), 152.
2. *Day by Day in God's Kingdom: A Discipleship Journal* can be downloaded from lifeway.com/masterlife.

WEEK 2

Truth and Faith

This Week's Goal

You will be able to explain the relationship between truth and faith. You will be able to exercise your faith, based on God's Word, to pray about a need or a problem.

My Walk with the Master This Week

You will complete the following activities to develop the six biblical disciplines. When you have completed each activity, draw a vertical line in the diamond beside it.

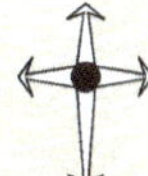

SPEND TIME WITH THE MASTER

◇ Have a quiet time each day. Check each day you have a quiet time: ☐ Sunday ☒ Monday ☒ Tuesday ☒ Wednesday ☒ Thursday ☒ Friday ☒ Saturday

LIVE IN THE WORD

◇ Read your Bible every day. Write what God says to you and what you say to God.
◇ Memorize 2 Timothy 3:16-17.
◇ Review 1 John 4:4.
◇ Read "How to Listen to God's Word."
◇ Use the Hearing the Word form with a Sunday School lesson, sermon, or CD.

PRAY IN FAITH

◇ Use "Guide to Praise" during your prayer time.
◇ Write prayer promises that apply to the requests on your Prayer-Covenant List.

FELLOWSHIP WITH BELIEVERS

◇ Identify the sources of help you receive from your church for spiritual warfare.
◇ Share with someone the Breastplate of Righteousness part of the Spiritual Armor.

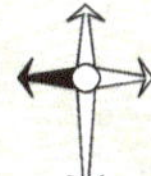

WITNESS TO THE WORLD

◇ List on the Relational-Witnessing Chart the names of lost persons.
◇ Make friends of non-Christians.

MINISTER TO OTHERS

◇ Learn the Breastplate of Righteousness part of the Spiritual Armor.

This Week's Scripture-Memory Verses

"All Scripture is God-breathed and is useful for teaching, rebuking, correcting and training in righteousness, so that the man of God may be thoroughly equipped for every good work" (2 Tim. 3:16-17).

Daily Master Communication Guide

Psalm 119:41-48

What God said to me:

Trust in my word and I will give you an answer for those who come against you. When you speak My word you will never be put to shame. I will never take My word from your mouth because you put your hope in my word.

What I said to God:

God I trust in your word, Help me to continue to learn and hold to your word. I believe you that when I speak your word, I will never be put to shame, so I will speak your word. thank you that you will not take your word from my mouth and please help me to continue to put my hope in you.

DAY 1

The Source of Truth

Don Dennis's problems began when he was a child. Both parents were alcoholics, and he repeatedly saw his father physically abuse his mother until they divorced. He was then sent to live with his grandparents. Don started drinking and taking drugs. When he was 16, he was sent to jail for the first of many times for writing bad checks and for armed robbery. At age 43 he received a life sentence as an incorrigible sociopath and was told that he would never get out of prison.

While Don was in prison, another prisoner sent him a note witnessing about his faith in God. He recalls: "I started reading in the New Testament that Jesus died for the downtrodden. I had thought that Jesus was only for righteous people, but I realized that Jesus was saying, 'I will forgive you.' I invited Jesus into my life and was baptized."

The truth from God's Word was crucial for the salvation of this inmate. This week's Scripture-memory verses speak of the importance of God's Word. Turn to page 27 and read this Scripture aloud to begin hiding it in your heart.

Three months after Don was baptized, the Washington state supreme court heard an appeal of his case, overturned his life sentence on a technicality, and released him on the basis of time served. A new set of problems began for Don when he tried to live the Christian life as a free man. He attended several churches, but his status as a former convict got in the way. Don explains: "People feared me. It made me resentful." Don said that misunderstandings between himself and church members frustrated his efforts to mature as a Christian. "I knew how to live for Jesus in a prison chapel, but I didn't know how to live for Him on the streets."

Don remembered a promise made by a man from Prison Fellowship that he would be glad to help him if Don were ever released. He moved Don into his home and helped him get a job, where Don met his future wife, Carol. They began to go to church and were invited to participate in a *MasterLife* group. Don said, "When I saw the Disciple's Cross, I finally understood how to internalize a structure that would help me deal with the world." Don grew fast as a Christian, and God called him to begin a prison ministry using *MasterLife* with prisoners during and after incarceration in the United States and overseas. The use of *MasterLife* in prisons has spread across the United States with an unusually high degree of success.

Just like Don Dennis, who struggled with Satan's ways and the Spirit's ways, every Christian must decide what is true. In spiritual warfare you must determine whether truth is what the world says or what God's Word says. Satan tries to make you doubt God's Word and listen to his lies. You must take up the Sword of the Spirit, which is His Word, and the Shield of Faith to help you walk by faith even when you cannot see the outcome. At the end of this week's study you will be able to—

- define *truth;*
- define *faith* by paraphrasing Hebrews 11:1;
- develop a plan for showing faith in action;
- explain the relationship between truth and faith.

THE TRUTH OF JESUS CHRIST

Read John 8:31-32 in the margin. In verse 32 Jesus spoke of His mission on earth: to communicate truth, the reality of God, to all people. To love the truth is to love Christ.

Answer these questions based on what you read in John 8:31-32.

Who is the source of truth? God/Jesus

What is the source of truth? God's teaching (continue in it, Follow Christ)

How should you react to the truth? Hold to the truth

What does spiritual truth do for you? Set you free from sin

In the spiritual sense truth is God's revelation of Himself to you. That truth is most clearly revealed in Jesus, the incarnate Word (read John 14:6 and 1 John 1:1-4 in the margin). The Bible is the written record of God's revelation. You react to the truth by continuing in it, or by following Christ. Continuing in that truth will set you free from sin's captivity. Acknowledging that Christ is the Savior and trusting in Him set you free from the fear of death. You are then free to believe that you will live forever with the Father.

Based on Romans 6:17-18, in the margin, from what are you freed?

Being a slave to sin.

Truth sets you free from the captivity of sin. The truth of Jesus Christ liberates people from sin and gives them eternal life.

The words "the truth will set you free" often appear over the entrances of universities and justice departments. They seem to signify that knowledge and understanding can make you free. Do you think this use of the phrase conveys the same meaning Jesus meant by it? ❑ Yes ☒ No Why?

They are speaking of earthly truth. Jesus means that He is the truth and we should know Him, and He will set us free.

"If you hold to my teaching, you are really my disciples. Then you will know the truth, and the truth will set you free" (John 8:31-32).

"Jesus answered, 'I am the way and the truth and the life. No one comes to the Father except through me' " (John 14:6).

"That which was from the beginning, which we have heard, which we have seen with our eyes, which we have looked at and our hands have touched—this we proclaim concerning the Word of life. The life appeared; we have seen it and testify to it, and we proclaim to you the eternal life, which was with the Father and has appeared to us. We proclaim to you what we have seen and heard, so that you also may have fellowship with us. And our fellowship is with the Father and with his Son, Jesus Christ. We write this to make our joy complete" (1 John 1:1-4).

"Thanks be to God, that though you used to be slaves to sin, you wholeheartedly obeyed the form of teaching to which you were entrusted" (Rom. 6:17-18).

All scripture is God breathed and is useful for teaching, rebuking correcting, and training in righteousness, so that the man of God may be thoroughly equipped for every good work.
2 Tim 3:16-17

When Jesus made this statement in John 8:32, He referred to the truth that represented God's revelation. This is the only kind of truth that can set people free from the clutches of sin.

PUTTING ON THE SPIRITUAL ARMOR

As you learned in week 1, putting on the Spiritual Armor is a key way to keep Satan from exerting his influence in your life. Turn to page 129 and review the Spiritual Armor presentation, with special emphasis on the Breastplate of Righteousness. By the end of this study you will be able to explain the entire presentation in your own words.

The Breastplate of Righteousness reminds you to do three things:

1. Ask God to search your heart to reveal any wicked ways in it.
2. Confess any sin.
3. Claim Christ's righteousness to cover your sins and to give you right standing with Him.

"Search me, O God,
and know my heart;
test me and know
my anxious thoughts.
See if there is any offensive
way in me,
and lead me in the way
everlasting (Ps. 139:23-24).

Focus on the first of the three reminders. Stop and ask God to search your heart to reveal any wicked ways in it. Read Psalm 139:23-24 in the margin.

Read Psalm 119:41-48 during your quiet time today. Let God speak to you through this passage. Then complete the Daily Master Communication Guide in the margin on page 28.

DAY 2

God's Truth Revealed

"You belong to your father, the devil, and you want to carry out your father's desire. He was a murderer from the beginning, not holding to the truth, for there is no truth in him. When he lies, he speaks his native language, for he is a liar and the father of lies" (John 8:44).

In day 1 you read about a major reversal in the direction of Don Dennis's life. This hardened criminal responded to the truth in God's Word, realized that he was lost in sin, was forgiven, and now has victory in Christ. Before that change, Don had listened to a different source, which had lied to him and had convinced him that thievery, alcohol, and other drugs were ways to meet his needs.

Read John 8:44 in the margin. Who is the source of lies? Devil

The opposite of truth is error, and Satan is its source. Satan's assault is aimed directly at God's truth. The ungodly boast of humanity's wisdom and self-sufficiency contradict that truth.

Read Romans 1:25 in the margin. What did Paul accuse the ungodly of doing?

☑ **Exchanging the truth of God for a lie**

❑ **Worshiping and serving the Creator**

"They exchanged the truth of God for a lie, and worshiped and served created things rather than the Creator—who is forever praised" (Rom. 1:25).

People who follow the world's ways and worship what the world offers exchange what God created for falsehood. The first statement above is the correct one.

As stated in *MasterLife 2: The Disciple's Personality,* a natural person is someone who is closed to the Spirit of God but is open to Satan's temptation and power. The natural person makes decisions on the basis of physical information and whatever logic or emotion the person attaches to it. The natural person gathers information through the senses and interprets this information with the mind. Sometimes the natural person's will, emotions, and sinful nature cause him or her to draw erroneous conclusions. At best, the natural person's personality is tied to the world and is under the influence of evil and error. As a result, this person cannot understand spiritual truth.

"The man without the Spirit does not accept the things that come from the Spirit of God, for they are foolishness to him, and he cannot understand them, because they are spiritually discerned" (1 Cor. 2:14).

Read 1 Corinthians 2:14 in the margin; then fill in the blanks: The man without the Spirit **does not accept the things that come from the** Spirit of God**, for they are** Foolishness **to him.**

DEMOLISHING PERSONAL SPIRITUAL STRONGHOLDS

Last week you focused on the stronghold of bitterness in your life. Today you will look at another stronghold mentioned in the Sermon on the Mount and will consider ways the Holy Spirit helps you build Christlike character as you work to demolish this stronghold.

"You have heard that it was said, 'Do not commit adultery.' But I tell you that anyone who looks at a woman lustfully has already committed adultery with her in his heart. If your right eye causes you to sin, gouge it out and throw it away. It is better for you to lose one part of your body than for your whole body to be thrown into hell. And if your right hand causes you to sin, cut it off and throw it away. It is better for you to lose one part of your body than for your whole body to go into hell" (Matt. 5:27-30).

Read the verses in the margin that deal with the stronghold of lust. Lust is a desire for what is forbidden—a desire for things that are contrary to God's will. Describe the area of lust in your life that needs to be demolished, what you need to do to demolish it, and the spiritual weapon(s) to be used in demolishing it. Later this week you will record your progress.

Here is an example.

Stronghold to be demolished: lust; difficulty resisting sexually explicit magazines that cause me to lust

What I need to do to demolish it: avoid looking at sexually explicit magazines on newsstands; destroy copies of pictures I have collected; review and obey John 8:31-32

"Those who belong to Christ Jesus have crucified the sinful nature with its passions and desires. Since we live by the Spirit, let us keep in step with the Spirit" (Gal. 5:24-25).

Spiritual weapons to be used: Helmet of Salvation—claim the mind of Christ; Breastplate of Righteousness—confront my sin; Sword of the Spirit—replace those thoughts with God's Word

Now you try it.

Stronghold to be demolished: ____________________

____

What I need to do to demolish it: ____________________

____

Spiritual weapon(s) to be used: ____________________

____

Christians can resist lust through the Holy Spirit's power. The flesh, with its passions and lusts, is to be crucified, as Galatians 5:24 states. The Holy Spirit gives you the ability to overcome the personal stronghold of lust and to bring it captive to Christ.

To help you deal with spiritual strongholds, God has given you His truth.

To help you deal with spiritual strongholds, God has given you His truth. Truth is reality God has chosen to reveal to you. You can discern spiritual truth for two reasons:

- You are born again of the Spirit. John 3:6 says, "Flesh gives birth to flesh, but the Spirit gives birth to spirit." Because you are born again, the Holy Spirit enables you to discern truth.
- God has given you His revealed Word.

What do this week's Scripture-memory verses, 2 Timothy 3:16-17, say about God's revealed Word and its functions in your life?

____

____

You may have answered like this: God's Word is revealed to me to equip me completely for every challenge of the Christian life.

How does God's Spirit convey spiritual truth to you? Circle two:

Through my spirit	**Through my flesh**
Through my body	**Through astrology**
Through the Bible	**Through direct revelation**

God reveals His truth to you so that you can know His will and His way. He conveys this to you through your spirit and through the Bible.

How do you know what God is revealing to you through His Word? One way is knowing how to listen as His Word is preached. You may hear excellent sermons week after week, yet you fail to understand how God may be speaking to you through them because you do not know how to process what you are hearing. The following guide may help you. If you have studied *MasterLife 2: The Disciple's Personality*, you may recognize this material, but read it again as a review.

HOW TO LISTEN TO GOD'S WORD

1. Evaluate what kind of hearer you are. Read Matthew 13:3-23 and classify yourself as one of the following.
   a. Apathetic hearer: hears the Word but is not prepared to receive and understand it (see v. 19).
   b. Superficial hearer: receives the Word temporarily but does not let it take root in the heart (see vv. 20-21).
   c. Preoccupied hearer: receives the Word but lets the worries of this world and the desire for things choke it (see v. 22).
   d. Reproducing hearer: receives the Word, understands it, bears fruit, and brings forth results (v. 23).
2. Be alert for a Word from God: (see Jas. 1:19, RSV).
3. Clear away all sin and pride so that the Word can be planted in your heart (see Jas. 1:21).
4. Pay attention to what the Bible says about you, just as you would to your reflection in a mirror (see Jas. 1:23).
   a. Take notes on the Hearing the Word form (see p. 141).
   b. Write the points of the message as the speaker presents them.
   c. Under each point write explanation, illustrations, and application.
   d. Write any specific statements the Spirit impresses on you.
   e. Summarize as soon as possible the main point the speaker wants you to do, be, and/or feel. Ask:
      - What did God say to me through this message?
      - How does my life measure up to this Word?
      - What actions will I take to bring my life in line with this Word?
      - What truth do I need to study further?
5. Do the Word, and you will be blessed in what you do (see Jas. 1:25).

Be alert for a Word from God.

Hearing the Word and learning to apply it to your life are key ways to demolish personal spiritual strongholds. Be a diligent hearer of the Word by using the Hearing the Word form provided on page 141. Copy and use this form so that taking notes will be a regular part of your life.

Hearing the Word and learning to apply it to your life are key ways to demolish personal spiritual strongholds.

Record on the Hearing the Word form what you learn from a Sunday School lesson, a sermon, or a CD.

Daily Master Communication Guide

Psalm 119:49-56

What God said to me:

I have given you my word so that you will have hope in me. I have given you my Word as a shield, comfort, strength, and a source of peace. Hide my words in your heart that you may be encouraged today.

What I said to God:

thank you God, for your word, your word that teaches, strengthens, keeps, and gives life. Thank you God for filling me up with your word everyday. Thank you God for understanding of your word, that I can use to encourage others.

STRENGTH FROM THE BODY OF CHRIST

The body of Christ is another source of help in spiritual warfare. In the body of Christ not only do you hear the Word preached and learn to apply it, but other Bible-believing Christians also hold you accountable for how you live in Christ and help strengthen you for the journey.

Attend worship services in your church and check the sources of help you receive from the body for spiritual warfare.

- ☒ **Hearing God's Word proclaimed and taught**
- ☒ **Fellowshipping with other Christians**
- ☒ **Having a group hold you accountable**
- ☒ **Being aware that other Christians have struggled as you do**
- ☒ **Having a group pray with you about a task, decision, or battle**
- ☒ **Ministering to and serving others**
- ☒ **Having Christian role models to emulate**
- ☐ **Other: ____________________**

Read Psalm 119:49-56 during your quiet time today. Then complete the Daily Master Communication Guide in the margin.

DAY 3

Encountering Satan's Lies

When we lived in Jember in East Java on our second term as missionaries, every street except one in this city of 75,000 people had a three-way intersection. You see, the people of Jember believed that everything has a spirit and that spirits cannot turn corners. If the city did not have a four-way intersection, then the spirit was stymied at that point. At the one four-way intersection, the police department was on one corner and the Catholic church on another.

One day my secretary, a well-educated Muslim, told me that her mother had back problems because she had once moved a heavy rock at the spring. The secretary said the spirit in the rock, unhappy that the rock had been moved, came to reside in her mother's back to plague her. Animists believe that they must give offerings to keep these spirits from annoying them.

These people's lives were governed by errors originated by Satan. Our job as missionaries was to teach the truth and proclaim God's power over all. But you do not have to serve in a foreign country to encounter Satan's lies in every area of life. Only the Holy Spirit can enable you to discern God's truth from Satan's half-truths and lies.

KNOWING SPIRITUAL TRUTH

According to John 8:31, in the margin, what is the best way to know spiritual truth?

"If you hold to my teaching, you are really my disciples" (John 8:31).

Hold to god's teachings

In John 16:13, in the margin, who is the Spirit of truth, who guides you into all truth?

"When he, the Spirit of truth, comes, he will guide you into all truth. He will not speak on his own; he will speak only what he hears, and he will tell you what is yet to come" (John 16:13).

Jesus Christ (the Holy spirit)

The Holy Spirit guides you into all truth and helps you discern what is truth as opposed to Satan's lies. The best way to know spiritual truth is to hold to Christ's teachings. According to Scripture, this obedience indicates that you are Christ's disciple.

Read 2 Timothy 2:15 in the margin. Underline the term Paul used to describe God's Word.

A workbook A course of study The Word of truth

"Do your best to present yourself to God as one approved, a workman who does not need to be ashamed and who correctly handles the word of truth" (2 Tim. 2:15).

Define *truth*, based on what you have read so far. Contrast it with error.

Truth is reality god has chosen to reveal to you. (the word of god)

The Word of God is the Word of truth. Carriers of God's truth are to represent that truth and its author unapologetically. Your job is to be a worker or craftsperson who correctly handles the Word of truth.

This week's Scripture-memory verses, 2 Timothy 3:16-17, underscore the way the Word of truth can equip you so that you never have to be ashamed of it. In the margin write your memory verses from one to three times.

All scripture is god breathed, and is useful for teaching, correcting, rebuking, and training in righteousness, so that the man of god may be thoroughly equipped for every good work
2 Tim 3:16-17

PUTTING ON THE SPIRITUAL ARMOR

In day 1 you learned the the Breastplate of Righteousness in the Spiritual Armor presentation. You studied three steps in putting on the Breastplate of Righteousness. Review them on page 30.

Focus on the second step in putting on the Breastplate of Righteousness. Stop and confess any sin that separates you from full fellowship with Christ.

Kerry Skinner, while serving as a church-staff member in Florida, used the Spiritual Armor to help a couple whose infant was seriously ill with

Daily Master Communication Guide

Psalm 119:57-64

What God said to me:

I am the surce of your happiness and blessings. Obay my words and you will enjoy this. I will fulfill every promise that I have made to you from the beginning of time.

What I said to God:

God I thank you for being the surce of my happiness and blessing. I pray that you will help me to know and understand this. God I believe that you will fulfill every promise you made to me. Please help me to continue to believe this. Amen.

meningitis. The couple, understandably fearful for the child's life, grew doubtful that God was present in the situation. Kerry explained the Spiritual Armor to the parents and helped them pray through the armor for their crisis. A couple who had lost three children overheard his conversation about the Spiritual Armor. Afterward, they took Kerry aside and told him that the Spiritual Armor was helpful to them. I pray that you will continue to find ways the Spiritual Armor will strengthen your walk and that of others, giving you victory over Satan.

What better way to arm yourself than through prayer? Read "Guide to Praise" and pray through it step by step in your prayer time.

GUIDE TO PRAISE

Praise and thanksgiving are two ways to glorify God, but each has a different focus. Praise is adoring God for who He is—His person, character, and attributes. Thanksgiving, which you studied last week, is expressing gratitude to God for what He has done—His actions. You may find it easier to give thanks than to praise, but a greater act of worship than thanking God for what He does is praising Him for who He is. Thanksgiving leads to praise. Thank God in everything and praise Him continually.

Why Should You Praise God?

1. God should be praised by His people (see Ps. 22:3; Rev. 19:5).
2. Praise is our gift (sacrifice) to God (see 1 Pet. 2:5; Heb. 13:15).
3. God saved us to glorify Him (see Isa. 43:21; Ps. 50:23).
4. Praise is commanded (see 1 Chron. 16:28-29; Ps. 147—150).
5. Praise prepares us for what we will do in heaven (see Rev. 5:9-14; 7:9-17).

How Should You Praise God?

1. Bless, glorify, praise, and adore God, using your own words.
2. Use scriptural prayers to glorify God.
3. Use spiritual songs, hymns, and scriptural melodies (see Eph. 5:18-19).
4. Use instruments to praise Him.
5. Recount God's glorious acts. This differs from thanksgiving in that it speaks of past acts as manifestations of God's glory.

What Should You Say When You Praise God?

1. Read aloud and pray the following prayers of praise and adoration.
   a. Glorify God's person, character, and attributes (see Ps. 8; 19; 24; 65; 92; 104; 139).
   b. Praise God's goodness (see Ps. 9; 30; 108; 138; Ex. 15:1-19; 1 Sam. 2:1-10; 1 Chron. 29:10-19; Luke 1:46-55).

c. Enjoin others to honor Him (see Luke 19:37-38; Eph. 3:20-21; 1 Tim. 1:17; Jude 25; Rev. 5:9-14; 7:9-12; 15:3-4; 19:1-7).

2. Use words of praise such as worship, adore, bless, exalt, magnify, laud, extol, glorify, and honor.

Praise Exclamations

- Hallelujah!
- Hosanna!
- Praise God!

When Should You Praise the Lord?
Continually!

When should you praise the Lord? Continually!

Where Should You Praise the Lord?
Everywhere!

Who Should Praise the Lord?
Everyone!

Read Psalm 119:57-64 during your quiet time today. Let God speak to you through this passage. Then complete the Daily Master Communication Guide in the margin on page 36.

DAY 4

Faith Grounded in Truth

When you have discerned the truth of God's Word, you have something in which to put your faith. The word *faith* is often misunderstood and misused. A child once defined *faith* as *believing something even when you know it isn't true.* That is not biblical faith. Faith is not blind allegiance that hopes against hope that something is true. Biblical faith is grounded in truth. God's Word is truth.

According to Romans 10:17, in the margin, from where does faith come?

"Faith comes from hearing the message, and the message is heard through the word of Christ" (Rom. 10:17).

Hearing the word of god.

People cannot hear the message unless the Word of Christ is proclaimed. Faith is their response when God's Word is revealed to them.

"Faith is being sure of what we hope for and certain of what we do not see" (Heb. 11:1).

SURE OF WHAT WE HOPE FOR

The words *being sure* in Hebrews 11:1, in the margin, can be translated *assurance*. This verse says that faith is *believing God's promises* as strongly as if they were already objective realities.

Which of these statements is a truer definition of *faith*?

- ☑ **Something God says is true but you cannot perceive with your senses**
- ❑ **Something you can perceive with your senses**

"When Jesus had entered Capernaum, a centurion came to him, asking for help. 'Lord,' he said, 'my servant lies at home paralyzed and in terrible suffering.' Jesus said to him, 'I will go and heal him.' The centurion replied, 'Lord, I do not deserve to have you come under my roof. But just say the word, and my servant will be healed. For I myself am a man under authority, with soldiers under me. I tell this one, "Go," and he goes; and that one, "Come," and he comes. I say to my servant, "Do this," and he does it.' When Jesus heard this, he was astonished and said to those following him, 'I tell you the truth, I have not found anyone in Israel with such great faith. I say to you that many will come from the east and the west, and will take their places at the feast with Abraham, Isaac and Jacob in the kingdom of heaven. But the subjects of the kingdom will be thrown outside, into the darkness, where there will be weeping and gnashing of teeth.' Then Jesus said to the centurion, 'Go! It will be done just as you believed it would.' And his servant was healed at that very hour" (Matt. 8:5-13).

Faith involves having absolute confidence in something without physical evidence. We can know God only when we have faith in what He says, since God is invisible. Your assurance comes as God reveals His will through His Word. Often, Christians try to manufacture faith by desperately trying to believe that something will happen. Their "faith" is based not on God's revealed will but on the desires of their hearts.

The account of Jesus' healing of the centurion's servant in Matthew 8:5-13, in the margin, is an example of true faith. When Jesus offered to heal the servant, the centurion believed that Jesus would do it. For this man, Jesus' promise of healing was a reality waiting to be claimed. The servant was healed immediately.

In Matthew 8:5-13 what was the basis of this man's faith?

- ❑ **The word of the Lord**
- ❑ **The desire of his heart**
- ❑ **A difference in his situation**

The man's actions were based on Jesus' assurance to him. When Jesus commanded him to go, assuring him that his servant would be healed, this promise came to pass. The centurion had such faith that he believed that the servant would be healed by Jesus' saying the words without even traveling to his home. The man's assurance occurred at the moment he heard and believed what the Lord said.

CERTAIN OF WHAT WE DO NOT SEE

The second part of Hebrews 11:1 says that faith is being "certain of what we do not see." The words *being certain* refer to a conviction. It has been said that while a belief is something you hold, a conviction is something that holds you.

Write a definition of *faith* by paraphrasing Hebrews 11:1: "Faith is being sure of what we hope for and certain of what we do not see."

Faith is the confidence in what we hope for and assurance about what we do not see.

Faith pleases God because it shows that we trust His promises even when they seem to be impossible. You may have written something like, Faith is being sure that something God promises is a reality.

Say aloud this week's Scripture-memory verses, 2 Timothy 3:16-17. Based on these verses, describe how you think God's Word thoroughly equips you to have faith in things you cannot see.

Teaches you, rebuke you, correct you, and train you.

As you have studied about faith and believing in things you cannot see, based on God's promises, maybe you have thought about requests on your Prayer-Covenant List. Has God revealed a promise from Scripture that you have claimed for some of those requests? As you learn about faith, you realize that God's Word is the basis for believing in things you cannot see.

Turn to your Prayer-Covenant List on page 143. Ask God to reveal a prayer promise about each item you have listed. When He does, write the prayer promise for each request on your list.

DEMOLISHING PERSONAL SPIRITUAL STRONGHOLDS

In day 2 you identified a stronghold you wanted to demolish in the area of lust. Today give a progress report on how you are using the spiritual weapon(s) you listed to demolish this stronghold.

How I am using a spiritual weapon(s) to demolish the stronghold of lust:

sword of the spirit- replacing these thoughts with God's word. Breastplate of righteousness- Confront the sin.

Continue to use "Guide to Praise," which you learned in day 3, during your quiet time this week.

Read Psalm 119:65-72 during your quiet time today. Let God speak to you through this passage. Then complete the Daily Master Communication Guide in the margin.

Daily Master Communication Guide

Psalm 119:65-72

What God said to me:

Trust the words that I have spoken and you will know the truth, the truth that will teach you and train you in the way you should go.

What I said to God:

Help me God please, to trust you with all of my heart and soul and mind. Help me to believe every word that you have spoken and will speak to me. Help me not to stray to the things of the world o God. Amen.

DAILY MASTER COMMUNICATION GUIDE

PSALM 119:73-80

What God said to me:

Put your hope in my word. Trust in me and you will noth be put to shame. I will give you under-standing of my word so that your faith in me will continue to grow

What I said to God:

thank you Lord for your precious words, your words of wisdom. I know O god that if I trust in you I will never be put to shame, so I trust in your word O god. thank you for giving me understanding of your word so that my faith in you will continue to grow.

DAY 5

Believing Without Seeing

Faith is being convinced that something is real because God said it, even though you cannot see it. Faith is possible even when your physical senses cannot prove the reality of something. In fact, *The Amplified Bible* says that faith is "the proof of things [we] do not see *and* the conviction of their reality—faith perceiving as real fact what is not revealed to the senses" (Heb. 11:1, AMP).

You do not have to see something to believe that it exists. You may not understand electricity; yet you still turn on the light when you enter a dark room. The reason you can believe without seeing is the evidence that the thing exists. You have never seen the Holy Spirit, but you can experience Him at work in your life and in the lives of others. You have not seen Jesus, but you know that He is present within you. Jesus told Thomas, "Blessed are those who have not seen, and yet have believed" (John 20:29). You can believe because the Holy Spirit reveals truth to you through God's Word.

This week's Scripture-memory verses, 2 Timothy 3:16-17, promise that God's Word can equip you for all things—including the steps of faith you take. Write these verses in the margin from one to three times. Also take this opportunity to review 1 John 4:4, the verse you memorized in week 1.

Write in your own words Hebrews 11:1: Faith is being "certain of what we do not see."

Faith is the confidence in what we hope for and assurance about what we do not see.

Faith is the conviction that something is real even though you cannot see it. Perhaps you wrote a similar statement.

FAITH IN ACTION

Hebrews 11:2 affirms that many persons in the Old Testament were noted for their faith. The remaining verses of Hebrews 11 records ways their lives demonstrated faith. This roll call of faith does not mention them merely because of what they thought. They are listed and praised because of their works of faith—their faith in *action.*

Faith is not just an intellectual belief or an emotional response. You show faith when you act on the revealed will of God. God's will is revealed in His Word. His Word says that your life should exercise faith.

In the margin read the Scriptures about faith. Then match the Scripture references with the summary statements.

A	**1. Matthew 21:22**	**a. Pray in faith.**
B	**2. Hebrews 11:3**	**b. Understand by faith.**
D	**3. Ephesians 2:8-9**	**c. Live by faith.**
C	**4. 2 Corinthians 5:7**	**d. Be saved by faith.**

"If you believe, you will receive whatever you ask for in prayer" (Matt. 21:22).

"By faith we understand that the universe was formed at God's command, so that what is seen was not made out of what was visible" (Heb. 11:3).

"It is by grace you have been saved, through faith—and this not from yourselves, it is the gift of God—not by works, so that no one can boast" (Eph. 2:8-9).

"We live by faith, not by sight" (2 Cor. 5:7).

Did you answer 1. a, 2., b, 3. d, 4.c? Faith in action uses God's Word to know and do God's will. To use God's Word effectively, become and remain familiar with it. Being familiar with the Word and hiding it in your heart will help you know the truth when Satan's lies confront you. What is your commitment to daily, personal Bible study?

Describe how you are doing in reading your Bible daily. How many of the past 11 days have you read your Bible since you began this study? 10

If you have not read your Bible for all of the past 11 days, describe what you will do to improve your consistency.

____

After you have learned to use God's Word to discern His will, your lifestyle will be to walk in faith. Faith is acting on God's revealed will.

Describe something God has recently revealed to you through His Word on which you are acting by faith.

If I trust in Him, I will not be put to shame.

Review by describing the relationship between truth and faith.

God's word is truth. By faith you believe God's word and act on His reality, even when you cannot physically see what you believe.

God's Word is truth—the truth revealed by God and not the lies revealed by the devil. The devil would like for you to believe that if you cannot see something, you cannot believe it. By faith you believe in God's Word and act on its reality, even when what you believe cannot be physically seen. Faith gives you victory over the devil's snares.

Faith gives you victory over the devil's snares.

PUTTING ON THE SPIRITUAL ARMOR

Focus again on the importance of wearing the Breastplate of Righteousness. Review on page 30 the three steps you learned for putting on the Breastplate of Righteousness.

"God made him who had no sin to be sin for us, so that in him we might become the righteousness of God" (2 Cor. 5:21).

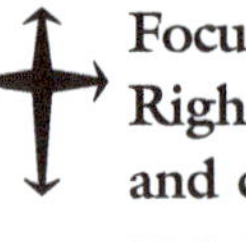

Focus on the third step in putting on the Breastplate of Righteousness. Read 2 Corinthians 5:21 in the margin. Stop and claim Christ's righteousness to cover your sins and give you right standing with Him. Ask Christ to forgive you and help you live a righteous life. Taking this step illustrates that you believe what God says even though you cannot see it.

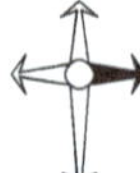

Share with your family, a Christian friend, or a group the Breastplate of Righteousness part of the Spiritual Armor.

Continue listing on the Relational-Witnessing Chart (p. 135) the names of persons who are not saved. Also write their names on the Prayer-Covenant List on page 143. Make friends with them and pray for them.

Over the next few days as you read the Word, be alert to Scriptures that relate to the requests on your Prayer-Covenant List. When you pray about that request, if you sense that God is impressing you to believe that scriptural promise, write it on your list. Do not make this just a routine action. The Holy Spirit needs to give you the faith to believe that a Scripture is God's promise to be applied to the problem. I write a need and a date in the margin of my Bible beside the promise that I sense God has given me for that need. As I read my Bible later, those promises become faith builders.

Read Psalm 119:73-80 during your quiet time today. Let God speak to you through this passage. Then complete the Daily Master Communication Guide in the margin on page 40.

HAS THIS WEEK MADE A DIFFERENCE?

Review "My Walk with the Master This Week" at the beginning of this week's material. Mark the activities you have finished by drawing vertical lines in the diamonds beside them. Finish any incomplete activities. Think about what you will say during your group session about your work on these activities.

Growing in your faith to believe God's promises can help you continue to replace Satan's strongholds in your life with Christlike character traits.

I hope that this study of "Truth and Faith" has made you aware of ways Satan tries to entrap you by making you doubt God's Word and things you cannot see or physically experience. Satan is never more unhappy than when you act on faith, because in that act you state your belief in God's promises rather than in Satan's lies. Growing in your faith to believe God's promises can help you continue to replace Satan's strongholds in your life with Christlike character traits. The Spiritual Armor gives you weapons to help you forge ahead when you need to walk by faith and not by sight.

WEEK 3

Rely on God's Word

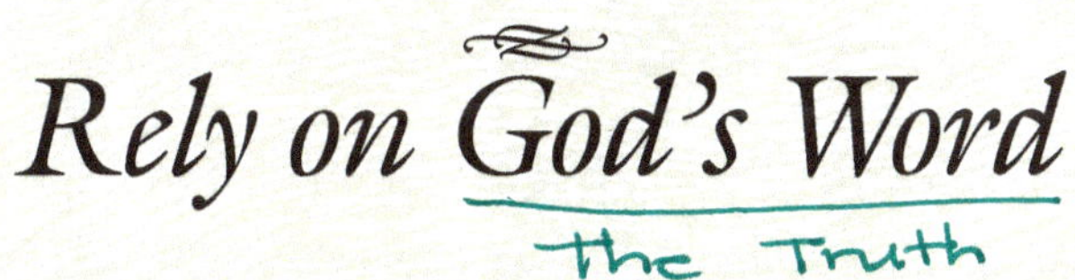

This Week's Goal

You will be able to depend on and use the Sword of the Spirit in spiritual warfare.

My Walk with the Master This Week

You will complete the following activities to develop the six biblical disciplines. When you have completed each activity, draw a vertical line in the diamond beside it.

SPEND TIME WITH THE MASTER

◇ Have a quiet time each day. Check each day you have a quiet time: ❑ Sunday ❑ Monday ❑ Tuesday ❑ Wednesday ❑ Thursday ❑ Friday ❑ Saturday

LIVE IN THE WORD

◇ Read your Bible every day. Write what God says to you and what you say to God.

◇ Read "How to Study God's Word."

◇ Memorize Psalm 1:2-3.

◇ Review 1 John 4:4 and 2 Timothy 3:16-17.

◇ Read the God's Word in Your Heart and Hand presentation.

PRAY IN FAITH

◇ Select an ideological stronghold and pray through the Spiritual Armor about it.

◇ Use "Guide to Confession and Forgiveness" during your prayer time.

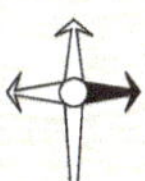

FELLOWSHIP WITH BELIEVERS

◇ Share with someone the Sword of the Spirit part of the Spiritual Armor.

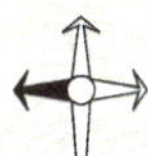

WITNESS TO THE WORLD

◇ List on the Relational-Witnessing Chart the names of lost persons.

◇ Begin using the witnessing booklet your leader gave you.

MINISTER TO OTHERS

◇ Learn the Sword of the Spirit part of the Spiritual Armor.

This Week's Scripture-Memory Verses

"His delight is in the law of the Lord,
and on his law he meditates day and night.
He is like a tree planted by streams of water,
which yields its fruit in season
and whose leaf does not wither.
Whatever he does prospers" (Ps. 1:2-3).

DAY 1

God's Reliable Word

God most often gives me guidance as I read through a book of the Bible one chapter at a time.

I have learned that God most often gives me guidance as I read through a book of the Bible one chapter at a time. I usually keep a list of questions or problems I am facing to refer to during my quiet time. At one time an agenda item was my need to find a successor to a retiring leader at the International Mission Board. I had been praying about this matter for several months when I went to Brazil to speak at a meeting of missionaries. Traveling with me were Ron Wilson, the area director for Brazil and the Caribbean, and John White, the treasurer of three missionary organizations represented at the meeting.

During the trip I read the next chapter in my Bible reading, Luke 19, in which Jesus told the parable of a nobleman who called his servants around him, gave them different amounts of money, and told them to put it to work. He was testing his servants to discover who could assume greater responsibility. That was what I was doing in seeking a replacement for the retiring leader. I knew that I needed to find a leader who could make long-range plans as well as build on past accomplishments.

Not knowing what I was thinking, Ron Wilson had remarked to me that John White was so industrious that Ron continually sought ways to challenge him. Ron commented that he believed one day John would have an even more responsible position. I began to see that my reading Luke 19 related to my enlisting the right person and that I needed to find out more about John White. John had been an assistant to Truett Cathy, the founder of the Chick-Fil-A restaurant chain, and had performed the same type of duties he would have in this position. With a doctor's degree in law and a master's degree in business administration, John possessed the skills that would be required for this position. In addition, John had been a missionary for 10 years and had pastored in Rio de Janeiro and Brasilia.

Ron Wilson told me that John had been the treasurer for one mission and had been given the responsibility of three missions. With his financial and administrative gifts and his experience as a missionary, he was well qualified to help me direct mission work around the world. Through the right Scripture at the right time, God led me to choose the right person to fill a major position. John's performance since then has confirmed that he was God's choice for the job.

Through the right Scripture at the right time, God led me to choose the right person to fill a major position.

Describe a time when God led you through His Word to make a crucial decision.

____

Your study this week will focus on various ways God's Word imparts truth so that you can overcome the enemy and can have victory in Christ. At the end of this week's study you will be able to—

- define the ways God's Word equips you to serve Him;
- study God's Word effectively.

THE STANDARD OF TRUTH

According to 2 Timothy 3:16-17, last week's Scripture-memory verses, what should be the basis of your standard for truth?

The word of God.

Why do these verses say that you can rely on Scripture for teaching as well as correcting and training?

The word of God never changes and is alway relevant "Alive and active".

Ministry that Christians perform needs to be based on the Bible. Scripture is God-breathed and therefore has authority for all correcting and training. It is the standard for truth and right.

Describe a time when you relied on sources other than God's Word to receive guidance for your life.

Going to colleges.

Standards are based on truth only when they are in line with God's Word. The inspired (God-breathed) Word is the only standard that stands the test of time. Our opinions and cultural priorities change, but the Word of God always endures. Read 1 Peter 1:24-25 in the margin.

"All men are like grass,
and all their glory is like
the flowers of the field;
the grass withers and the
flowers fall,
but the word of the Lord
stands forever"
(1 Pet. 1:24-25).

In 2 Timothy 3:16-17, in the margin, underline the four areas Scripture can be used for. Draw a star beside the area with which you feel you have the least experience.

Scripture is useful for teaching, rebuking, correcting, and training in righteousness. You may believe that areas involving doctrinal issues are the ones in which you have the most need for instruction. A Scripture may have rebuked you about an evil practice. You may need the Scripture to help you examine ways to live rightly and to hold you accountable for sinful behavior. You may have experienced Scripture correcting your direction back to the right path. You may have experienced scriptural training in right living. God's Word is authoritative in all areas of ministry because God is its source. This week you will study in depth these four ways Scripture can be used.

"All Scripture is God-breathed
and is useful for teaching,
rebuking, correcting and
training in righteousness, so
that the man of God may be
thoroughly equipped for every
good work" (2 Tim. 3:16-17).

Daily Master Communication Guide

Psalm 119:81-88

What God said to me:

Put your hope (Trust) in me and you will never fail. No matter what is happening around you or to you, I will always be there to guide and shield you. Do not give up on me or my word.

What I said to God:

I will put my trust in you O god because I know that you will never fail me. I know O god that you will always be there when I need you, please help me to remember this. Thank you Lord. Amen.

Begin working on this week's Scripture-memory verses, Psalm 1:2-3, which focus on the importance of God's Word. Turn to page 43 and read them aloud.

Learning how to study the Bible will make it easier for you to obtain all God wants to provide for you in His Word. Examine the following guidelines for studying the Word.

HOW TO STUDY GOD'S WORD

Many methods of Bible study exist:

- Studying a theme of the Bible
- Studying a book of the Bible
- Studying a passage in the Bible
- Studying a Bible word

The Bible is about God more than about people. However, the Bible is filled with people's stories. Whether they interacted with Him positively or negatively, God included them to teach us through examples from real life. Bible characters show God's principles as expressed in human experience. Studying a Bible character encourages you to apply God's principles to your life.

Choose a Bible character and discover what God teaches you through this person's life.

1. Gather basic information about the character:
   - Genealogy: what shaped the person's formative years?
   - Geography: where was the person born?
   - Significant events in the person's life
   - How the person responded to events
   - What other characters were this person's contemporaries
   - Statements the character made and what others said about this person
   - What impact the person had on others
   - The person's strengths and weaknesses
   - Evidence of the person's devotion to the Lord
2. Establish a lifeline for the Bible character and document with Scripture.
3. Write biblical principles you learn from the character's life. Read in one sitting all the Bible has to say about the character and draw lessons from his or her life.
4. Apply the teaching to your life. What strengths or weaknesses do you share with the person? Can you identify with this person's temptations and victories? Ask God to help you incorporate the truths you have learned from this character to make you a better disciple.

Read Psalm 119:81-88 during your quiet time today. Let God speak to you through this passage. Then complete the Daily Master Communication Guide on page 46.

DAY 2

The Basis of All Teaching

Yesterday you learned that God's Word is profitable in four specific ways. Today you will focus on the first of these, shown below in bold type:

1. teaching
2. rebuking
3. correcting
4. training in righteousness

GOD'S WORD TEACHES

The Phillips translation of 2 Timothy 3:16-17, the verse you are studying, uses the term "teaching the faith." Sometimes false doctrines steal into our lives. Someone may say that Jesus did not really have a human nature. Another person may say that Jesus did not actually die on the cross but only fainted. Satan can use your ignorance and false beliefs to bring you under attack. In contrast to lies and false teachings, we can rely on God's Word, which is absolutely true and totally dependable.

Teaching is preventative. Biblical instruction and guidance are designed to prevent a problem or to help a person correct it. If you are grounded in truth, you have God's Word as a point of reference when Satan tempts you to stray, and you can have victory.

"I have been reminded of your sincere faith, which first lived in your grandmother Lois and in your mother Eunice and, I am persuaded, now lives in you also" (2 Tim. 1:5).

Describe a time when proper instruction in God's Word prevented you from making a harmful decision.

Proverbs 15:1 prevents me from getting myself in situation where I become or make someone very angry.

Teaching is the primary way Jesus communicated with His disciples.

"From infancy you have known the holy Scriptures, which are able to make you wise for salvation through faith in Christ Jesus. All Scripture is God-breathed and is useful for teaching, rebuking, correcting, and training in righteousness, so that the man of God may be thoroughly equipped for every good work" (2 Tim. 3:15-17).

Read 2 Timothy 1:5 and 2 Timothy 3:15-17 in the margin. How was Timothy taught God's Word?

His mother and grandmother

Evidently, Timothy's mother and grandmother taught him. Who have been influential teachers in your life? List several.

Faith, Mr. Keller,

What was the result of Timothy's being taught the Scriptures?

Timothy recieved Christ and now he can go out and do God's work.

They led him to salvation, and now, Paul says, they will equip Timothy for every good work. The Bible is the ultimate source of all teaching. Reading it and applying its precepts prepare people for salvation because they call people to believe in Jesus.

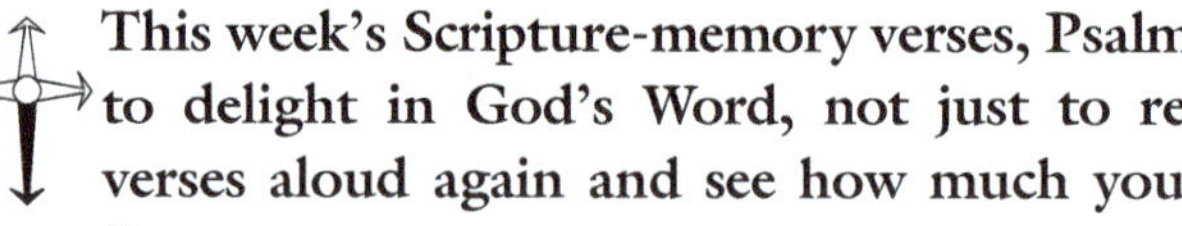

This week's Scripture-memory verses, Psalm 1:2-3, urge you to delight in God's Word, not just to read it. Read the verses aloud again and see how much you can already say from memory.

I hope that you are developing such a hunger and thirst for the Scriptures that you genuinely feel that your day is not complete until you have spent time in the Word.

DEMOLISHING PERSONAL SPIRITUAL STRONGHOLDS

In the past two weeks you focused on personal spiritual strongholds in your life. Today you will look at another stronghold mentioned in the Sermon on the Mount and will consider ways the Holy Spirit helps you build Christlike character as you demolish it.

"You have heard that it was said to the people long ago, 'Do not break your oath, but keep the oaths you have made to the Lord.' But I tell you, Do not swear at all: either by heaven, for it is God's throne; or by the earth, for it is his footstool; or by Jerusalem, for it is the city of the Great King. And do not swear by your head, for you cannot make even one hair white or black. Simply let your 'Yes' be 'Yes,' and your 'No,' 'No'; anything beyond this comes from the evil one" (Matt. 5:33-37).

"The tongue also is a fire, a world of evil among the parts of the body. It corrupts the whole person, sets the whole course of his life on fire, and is itself set on fire by hell" (Jas. 3:6).

"Reckless words pierce
like a sword,
but the tongue of the
wise brings healing"
(Prov. 12:18).

"The things that come out of the mouth come from the heart, and these make a man unclean" (Matt. 15:18).

Read the verses in the margin, which deal with the stronghold of harmful speech. People can use the tongue to bring glory to the Lord or to utter caustic, poisonous words. Satan can use the tongue to destroy you and others. [Possible strongholds of improper speech are exaggeration, swearing for emphasis, lying, using big words to strengthen your argument, hurtful criticism, and profanity.] Describe the area of improper speech in your life that needs to be demolished, what you need to do to demolish it, and the spiritual weapon(s) to be used in demolishing it. Later this week you will record your progress.

Here is an example.

Stronghold to be demolished: taking God's name in vain to strengthen the impact of what I am saying

What I need to do to demolish it: learn more effective ways to communicate so that I can reveal my true feelings without using words that hurt God and others

Spiritual weapons to be used: Sword of the Spirit—replace my desire to say more than I should by reading what the Scripture says about improper language; Breastplate of Righteousness—confess my sin and begin to live rightly

Now you try it.

Stronghold to be demolished: Lying

What I need to do to demolish it: Build up my courage to speak the truth even if it gets me in trouble, God will be right there to cover me.

Spiritual weapon(s) to be used: Sword of the Spirit - quiet my urge to lie by reading what the Scripture says about lying. Breastplate of righteousness - confess my sin and begin to live rightly.

* The tongue reflects a person's spirit; it reveals what is in the heart. Satan is pleased when you do not guard your tongue, because you demonstrate that he, not Christ, controls you.

Reread James 3:6, Proverbs 12:18, and Matthew 15:18 in the margin on page 48. Then match their references below with the statements that describe what the tongue is capable of doing.

B 1. James 3:6	**a. Reveals what is in the heart**
C 2. Proverbs 12:18	**b. Destroys the course of one's life**
A 3. Matthew 15:18	**c. Brings healing**

* The tongue is capable of both good and evil. It can bring healing, redirect the course of a person's life, or reveal the depravity of someone's heart. The correct answers are 1. b, 2. c, 3. a.

Read Psalm 119:89-96 during your quiet time today. Then complete the Daily Master Communication Guide in the margin.

Daily Master Communication Guide

Psalm 119:89-96

What God said to me:

People may fail you, and things may fail you, but my word will never fail. My word is everlasting and will stand the test of time. My word is the one constant thing in this ever changing world, that's why you should hold to my word.

What I said to God:

Thank you God for the comfort in knowing that no matter what is happening in life, your word will always be there to guide, teach, and keep me. Thank you for confidence and the ability to hold onto your word God. Amen.

DAY 3

Straying from the Way

How do you know when you are living outside God's standards? How do you know when you have drifted from right living? God's Word is the standard against which you measure yourself. God's Word can reach out and pull you back onto the path if you have strayed from the way.

Today you will study the second of the four specific ways God's Word is profitable for you, shown below in bold type.

1. teaching
2. **rebuking**
3. correcting
4. training in righteousness

GOD'S WORD REBUKES

A rebuke is a reproof that brings conviction, an awareness that you have done wrong. As you have read the Scriptures in the past, has a verse ever seemed to jump out to identify a way you have strayed? For example, you may be reading in Matthew 5 and reach the verse "Love your enemies and pray for those who persecute you" (Matt. 5:44). Suddenly, you feel that this verse has flashing neon lights around it. You say to yourself: *He's talking to me! I haven't loved and prayed for my enemies. Instead, I've been wishing them ill.* When that happens, it is no coincidence. The Lord is identifying a weakness in you. This is a wake-up call from the Scriptures telling you to get back in line with God's will and ways.

Describe a time when a verse of Scripture seemed to convict you that you had strayed from the right way of living.

Matthew 7, judging others and not realizing that I will judged in the same way.

Scriptural rebuke gives you guidance. It makes you aware that you are traveling in the opposite direction you should be going—that Satan has misled you. Through a verse of Scripture the Lord seems to say, "Here is the way; turn around from the way you are going and walk in the truth."

The Bible speaks of rebuke in a variety of situations. Read the verses in the margin that contain rebukes. Then match the references on the next page with the statements describing situations in which a rebuke is to be used.

"If anyone does not obey our instructions in this letter, take special note of him. Do not associate with him, in order that he may feel ashamed. Yet do not regard him as an enemy, but warn him as a brother" (2 Thess. 3:14-15).

"Those who sin are to be rebuked publicly, so that the others may take warning. I charge you, in the sight of God and Christ Jesus and the elect angels, to keep these instructions without partiality, and to do nothing out of favoritism" (1 Tim. 5:20-21).

"If your brother sins against you, go and show him his fault, just between the two of you. If he listens to you, you have won your brother over" (Matt. 18:15).

"He sent messengers on ahead, who went into a Samaritan village to get things ready for him; but the people there did not welcome him, because he was heading for Jerusalem. When the disciples James and John saw this, they asked, 'Lord, do you want us to call fire down from heaven to destroy them?' But Jesus turned and rebuked them, and they went to another village" (Luke 9:52-55).

___ 1. 2 Thessalonians 3:14-15	**a. When the person sinning is in a position of leadership that will cause others to stray**
___ 2. 1 Timothy 5:20-21	**b. When the person will not respond to the teaching of sound doctrine**
___ 3. Matthew 18:15	**c. When a person needs to be shocked into realizing his or her spiritual dullness or lack of understanding**
___ 4. Luke 9:52-55	**d. When a person does not realize or does not admit that he or she is living contrary to the truth**
___ 5. John 14:9-10	**e. When a person has a wrong spirit**

"Jesus answered, 'Don't you know me, Philip, even after I have been among you such a long time? Anyone who has seen me has seen the Father. How can you say, 'Show us the Father'? Don't you believe that I am the Father, and that the Father is in me?' " (John 14:9-10).

God's Word contains all you need to show you the way when Satan influences you to sin. The statements you read indicate times when the teachings of Scripture were used for rebuke or reproof. The correct answers are 1. b, 2. a, 3. d, 4. e, 5. c. Scripture is used to rebuke a wrong behavior or a wrong belief.

PUTTING ON THE SPIRITUAL ARMOR

This week's study underscores the importance of taking up the Sword of the Spirit, which is God's Word, as part of the Spiritual Armor. Turn to page 129 and review the Spiritual Armor presentation, with special emphasis on the Sword of the Spirit. By the end of this study you will be able to explain the entire presentation in your own words.

The Sword of the Spirit reminds you to do three things:

1. Grasp the Word. Use it whether or not the enemy acknowledges that it is God's Word.
2. Let the Holy Spirit use the Word. It is His sword.
3. Pray on the basis of the Word. The Spirit will use the Word to reveal God's will to you and to help you know what to pray for and do.

Focus on the first of the three reminders. Be prepared to use God's Word when you face an attack by Satan. When you feel that the enemy is tempting you, search your heart for God's Word, which you have hidden there, to remind you how you are to respond. Read Hebrews 4:12 in the margin.

"The word of God is living and active. Sharper than any double-edged sword, it penetrates even to dividing soul and spirit, joints and marrow; it judges the thoughts and attitudes of the heart" (Heb. 4:12).

GOD'S WORD IN YOUR HEART AND HAND

The hand in which you grasp the Word can be used to show several levels of Bible awareness and Bible study and to illustrate the importance of dwelling on the truths of God's Word. To keep Christ at the center

DAILY MASTER COMMUNICATION GUIDE

PSALM 119:97-104

What God said to me:

Meditate on my word in order to let it sink into your heart. The more time you spend in my word, the more my word will be in you. My word is all that you need to get you where I need you to be.

What I said to God:

Thank you O God for your direction. Thank you for your words of wisdom. Please help me to spend more time in your word. When I find time to engage in other things, please remind me of your word.

of your life, you need God's Word in your heart. As you pray through the Spiritual Armor, imagine grasping God's Word, the Sword of the Spirit, as you fight spiritual battles.

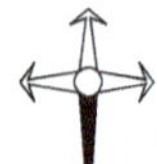

Read the God's Word in Your Heart and Hand presentation on pages 132–34.

Continue to hide the Word in your heart. In the margin on page 51 write from memory this week's Scripture-memory verses, Psalm 1:2-3. Then say aloud your memory verses from weeks 1 and 2.

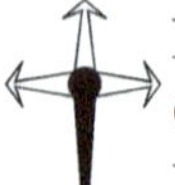

Read Psalm 119:97-104 during your quiet time today. Let God speak to you through this passage. Then complete the Daily Master Communication Guide in the margin.

DAY 4

Resetting Your Direction

As you learned in day 3 about rebuke, God's Word is useful to remind you when the rudder of the ship is steering the ship in the wrong direction—when God intends for you to pursue one course of action, but you are doggedly pursuing another. But Scripture is also useful for those who are not going in the opposite direction but have strayed from the path. The longer they go off course, the farther they move from the right way. They need a slight change of direction to get back on course before they go so far that rebuke is necessary.

Isaiah 30:21 says, "Whether you turn to the right or to the left, your ears will hear a voice behind you, saying, 'This is the way; walk in it.' " In 2 Timothy 3:16-17 you learned four specific ways God's Word keeps you on course. The third way appears below in bold type.

1. teaching
2. rebuking
3. **correcting**
4. training in righteousness

GOD'S WORD CORRECTS

God's Word profits a person or a church that needs to be corrected. It corrects your sins and failures. The word *correct* comes from a Greek word that means *to restore*. The Phillips translation of the Bible translates the term as "resetting the direction of a man's life." Correction is a Word from God that causes you to get back on the right track.

When do you need to reset your direction? Perhaps you read Matthew 6:19-34 and feel this passage speaks a Word of correction to you, making you aware that you have spent your life amassing earthly goods instead of laying up treasures in heaven. In this case the direction of your life could be reset because of an encounter with God's Word.

Read the Scriptures in the margin about times when a Word from the Lord was used to correct. Then match their references with the reasons the correction was needed.

C 1. Matthew 19:13-14 — **a. For making someone aware that he or she is acting contrary to his or her best interests**

A 2. Luke 9:49-50 — **b. For getting someone back on the proper course**

B 3. 2 Timothy 2:24-25 — **c. When someone does not understand the Kingdom**

"Little children were brought to Jesus for him to place his hands on them and pray for them. But the disciples rebuked those who brought them. Jesus said, 'Let the little children come to me, and do not hinder them, for the kingdom of heaven belongs to such as these' " (Matt. 19:13-14).

" 'Master,' said John, 'we saw a man driving out demons in your name and we tried to stop him, because he is not one of us.' 'Do not stop him,' Jesus said, 'For whoever is not against you is for you' " (Luke 9:49-50).

"The Lord's servant must not quarrel; instead, he must be kind to everyone, able to teach, not resentful. Those who oppose him he must gently instruct, in the hope that God will grant them repentance leading them to a knowledge of the truth, and that they will come to their senses and escape from the trap of the devil, who has taken them captive to do his will" (2 Tim. 2:24-25).

God's correction of you is motivated by love. When you have Christ at the center of your life, you need to have your direction properly set. It would be impossible to be an intimate disciple of Christ if you strayed from the path. The correct answers to the exercise are 1. c, 2. a, 3. b.

PUTTING ON THE SPIRITUAL ARMOR

In day 3 you reviewed the importance of the Sword of the Spirit in the Spiritual Armor presentation. You learned three guidelines for taking up the Sword of the Spirit. Review them on page 51.

Focus on the second guideline for taking up the Sword of the Spirit. Stop and ask the Holy Spirit to bring the Word to mind as you carry out your daily activities and need a reminder of how you should live, even if the Word brings correction to your life.

Say aloud this week's Scripture-memory verses, Psalm 1:2-3. What occurs when a person delights in the Word and allows it to correct him or her when necessary?

His leaf also shall not wither and whatsoever he doeth shall prosper.

When a person delights in the Word, then the correction that springs from the Word will be welcome. Such a person will not wither in the time of temptation and trial and will prosper.

Have you become more aware of your sins as you have just studied about correction from the Word? God offers forgiveness and fellowship with Him through confession. When you feel a barrier between you and God, use the following guide to discover and confess any sin that may be blocking the way.

As you pray today, follow the instructions in "Guide to Confession and Forgiveness."

GUIDE TO CONFESSION AND FORGIVENESS

God wants you to walk in the light and to have fellowship with Him and with other Christians (see 1 John 1:5-10).

Ask the Holy Spirit to Convict You of Sins

See John 16:8-11.

1. Do not try to convict yourself or to become involved in morbid introspection.
2. Ask God to search your heart, thoughts, and ways (see Ps. 139:23-24).
3. Let the Holy Spirit use the Word to show you how God views your heart, thoughts, and ways (see Rom. 8:26-27; Heb. 4: 12-13).
   a. Read your Bible daily.
   b. Read special passages as you feel the need.

Let the Holy Spirit use the Word to show you how God views your heart, thoughts, and ways.

Agree with God About the Seriousness of Your Sins

1. To confess, agree with God. The word confess means to agree with or admit. Do not try to excuse your behavior but accept what God convicts you of (see 1 John 1:8-10).
2. To confess, walk in the light of His holiness (see 1 John 1:7). Do not compare yourself to someone else to try to walk in that person's light.
3. To confess, be honest with God (see 1 John 1:8-10). Do not hide anything from God or from yourself.

Acknowledge Christ as the Atoning Sacrifice for Your Sins

See 1 John 2:1-2.

1. Express your sorrow and repentance to God (see Ps. 51).
2. Ask for forgiveness based on the blood of Christ, which cleanses us from all sin (1 John 1:7; 2:2). Do not base your request on works of righteousness you have done in the past or plan to do in the future (see Titus 3:5).
3. Turn over your sins to your advocate, Christ (see Heb. 4:14,16; 7:25; 9:24-26; 10:19,22; 1 John 2:2). Do not consider your sins again. Because God has forgiven you, consider those sins to be history.

Ask for forgiveness based on the blood of Christ.

Walk in the Light with Other Christians

See 1 John 1:7.

1. Be honest with other Christians about your sins. To walk in the light is to be open and honest (see 1 John 1:7).
2. Confess your sins to other understanding Christians as needed (see Jas. 5:16).

a. Confess during prayer with other believers.
b. Confess only to those who can help bear your burden in the spirit of humility (see Gal. 6:1). They should be persons who can keep a confidence and can help you overcome temptation.
c. Tell others only what is necessary. On some occasions you need to confess only that you have sinned and that God has forgiven you. At other times you may confess the sin but not the details. (If your confession relates to sexual impurity, do not go into detail. If you need to discuss details, do so with your pastor or a trained counselor.) If your sin is known or affects the church, ask others to forgive you as God has.
d. Confess only your sin, not someone else's. Do not blame anyone for your sin. Accept your part of the responsibility and do not implicate others.

3. Renounce your sin and make restitution if possible (see Luke 19:8). Any restitution is not to be considered penance and in no way pays for your sin. It is not done to relieve any guilt feelings, because Christ has already forgiven you. Yet restitution helps restore anything you have taken from another person and may witness to that person.

Restitution helps restore anything you have taken from another person and may witness to that person.

Walk in the Light with Christ
See 1 John 1:7.

1. When you sin again, confess immediately and ask God to forgive you.
2. Do not give up your struggle to be free from a sin you repeatedly commit. Satan will try to convince you that God will not forgive you for committing the same sin again. Of course, genuine repentance and turning from sin are necessary for you to receive forgiveness. However, sometimes you sin again in spite of your good intentions. If you seek forgiveness in genuine repentance, God will forgive you again. He will do for you as much as Jesus asked Peter to do: "If he sins against you seven times in a day, and seven times comes back to you and says, 'I repent,' forgive him" (Luke 17:4).
   a. Be careful that you do not sin because you know that you can ask to be forgiven. God does not play games. If you willfully sin, you treat lightly Christ's sacrifice for you.
   b. If you continually commit the same sin, counsel with your pastor or a trained Christian counselor.
3. Sin in a Christian's life does not change the person's relationship as a child of God, but it creates a barrier to fellowship with Him.

Forgiveness is God's gift. Confession and repentance are the God-ordained ways to free you from sin's penalty, presence, and power. Although you never reach perfection in this world, through Christ you can continually walk in the light with our holy God.

Confession and repentance are the God-ordained ways to free you from sin's penalty, presence, and power.

DAILY MASTER COMMUNICATION GUIDE

PSALM 119:105-112

What God said to me:

Let my word be what orders your steps and guides your feet. Whatever you do today and forever more should be based on my word and nothing else. If you follow my word, you will not go astray.

What I said to God:

thank you o god for you word that guides and leads. Thank you o god for keeping me on your right path, even when I stray. Thank you for always speaking to me and revealing your word to me.

As you read "Guide to Confession and Forgiveness," if you had a question about whether you have made that initial confession of your sins and experienced salvation, you can receive Jesus Christ now by inviting Him into your heart. Romans 10:13 says, "Everyone who calls on the name of the Lord will be saved." If you wish, use this prayer to express your commitment:

> *Lord Jesus, I need You. I am a sinner. I want You to be my Savior and my Lord. I accept Your death on the cross as the payment for my sins, and I now entrust my life to Your care. Thank You for forgiving me and for giving me a new life. Please help me grow in my understanding of Your love and power so that my life will bring glory and honor to You. Amen.*

Signed ______________ Date 04/15/22

I hope that you do not feel awkward if you began this study thinking that you were a Christian, only to realize that you had never fully given your heart and life to Christ. Often, as people learn through *MasterLife* what it means to commit their lives to Christ, they become aware that they have not taken this crucial first step.

Read Psalm 119:105-112 during your quiet time today. Let God speak to you through this passage. Then complete the Daily Master Communication Guide in the margin.

DAY 5

Thoroughly Equipped

When you studied the Breastplate of Righteousness, you learned that you were to keep the breastplate firmly fastened in place with upright character and righteous living. But how do you know what is involved in righteous living? In learning the Spiritual Armor, you read Psalm 66:18:

> *If I had cherished sin in my heart,*
> *the Lord would not have listened.*

You may yearn to live rightly and to remove yourself from a situation in which your heart cherishes sin. But how do you know what thoughts to avoid? How do you know how to separate yourself from wrong?

God's Word supplies ample instruction for how to live. Everything you need for guidance is contained in the Bible. You have been learning four ways the Scriptures benefit you. Today you will focus on the last way, shown below in bold type.

1. teaching
2. rebuking
3. correcting
4. **training in righteousness**

GOD'S WORD INSTRUCTS IN RIGHTEOUSNESS

Instruction in righteousness is more than just rearing a child or learning how to discipline. The Bible teaches moral character—how to live life rightly. The Phillips translation of 2 Timothy 3:16-17 says that the Bible is profitable for "training … in good living."

In Galatians 5:19-26, in the margin, underline with one line the things you are to put off. Underline with two lines the Spirit's ways a Christian is to add to his or her life.

"The acts of the sinful nature are obvious: sexual immorality, impurity and debauchery; idolatry and witchcraft; hatred, discord, jealousy, fits of rage, selfish ambition, dissensions, factions and envy; drunkenness, orgies, and the like. I warn you, as I did before, that those who live like this will not inherit the kingdom of God. But the fruit of the Spirit is love, joy, peace, patience, kindness, goodness, faithfulness, gentleness and self-control. Against such things there is no law. Those who belong to Christ Jesus have crucified the sinful nature with its passions and desires. Since we live by the Spirit, let us keep in step with the Spirit. Let us not become conceited, provoking and envying each other" (Gal. 5:19-26).

As a Christian you are not left to guess which way is right. Again and again the Bible instructs you in the practical, day-to-day ways to live.

Describe a time when you found the Bible useful in instructing you how to act in a specific situation.

Proverbs 15:1 → speaking with someone about something that needed to be dealt with, but didn't want the situation to be negative.

You are learning about this use of the Bible when you work on demolishing personal spiritual strongholds in your life.

DEMOLISHING PERSONAL SPIRITUAL STRONGHOLDS

In day 2 you identified a stronghold you wanted to demolish in the area of speech. Today give a progress report on how you have used the spiritual weapon(s) you listed to demolish this stronghold.

How I have used a spiritual weapon(s) to help demolish the stronghold of improper speech:

Allowing scripture to empower me to be bold in speaking the truth, no matter what the outcome will be.

Select an ideological stronghold such as gambling, pornography, humanism, or secularism. Then pray through the Spiritual Armor about its influence in your personal life and in society.

"All Scripture is God-breathed and is useful for teaching, rebuking, correcting and training in righteousness, so that the man of God may be thoroughly equipped for every good work" (2 Tim. 3:16-17).

What happens when you use the Scriptures in the four ways you have studied—for teaching, rebuking, correcting, and training in righteousness? Read 2 Timothy 3:16-17 in the margin and check the correct response.

If I rely on the Scriptures in these four ways, I will—
- ❑ **never sin again;**
- ❑ **never have problems;**
- ☒ **be equipped for how God wants me to live;**
- ❑ **have plenty of money.**

Scripture equips you for all you do. Being well grounded in God's Word does not guarantee that you will never have problems and that you will have all the money you want. It does not mean that you will not sin, because all human beings are sinful and are bound to stray. But you can rely on Scripture to give you victory in troubled times; to help keep you from giving in to Satan's attacks; and to show you ways your needs, even monetary ones, can be supplied.

By now you should have memorized this week's Scripture-memory verses, Psalm 1:2-3. Say them aloud to a friend or a family member. Ask this person to check the verses for you.

PUTTING ON THE SPIRITUAL ARMOR

Continue to study the importance of using the Sword of the Spirit in spiritual warfare as part of the Spiritual Armor. Review on page 51 the three guidelines for taking up the Sword of the Spirit.

"When he, the Spirit of truth, comes, he will guide you into all truth. He will not speak on his own; he will speak only what he hears, and he will tell you what is yet to come. He will bring glory to me by taking from what is mine and making it known to you. All that belongs to the Father is mine. That is why I said the Spirit will take from what is mine and make it known to you" (John 16:13-15).

Focus on the third guideline. Stop and pray on the basis of the Word. The Holy Spirit will guide you into all truth and will help you know how to pray even if you do not have a particular agenda in mind (read John 16:13-15 in the margin). Allow the Spirit to bring God's Word to mind as you pray.

Share with your family, a Christian friend, or a group the Sword of the Spirit part of the Spiritual Armor.

As you delight in God's Word, you naturally think of persons who do not have this Guidebook as a daily part of their lives. Earlier this week you listed on your Relational-Witnessing Chart the names of lost family members and relatives. Today you will focus on other lost individuals in your circles of influence.

List the names of lost persons in each circle on the Relational-Witnessing Chart (p. 135) and on the Prayer-Covenant List (p. 143).

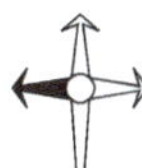
Begin using the witnessing booklet your leader gave you at the previous group session. Use one of the following suggestions to introduce the booklet to someone.

- **I have a booklet that means a lot to me. May I share it with you?**
- **May I share a booklet with you that explains how you can know for certain that you have eternal life?**
- **This booklet has a wonderful message about how to have a full and meaningful life. May I share it with you?**

Read Psalm 119:113-120 during your quiet time today. Let God speak to you through this passage. Then complete the Daily Master Communication Guide in the margin.

HAS THIS WEEK MADE A DIFFERENCE?

Review "My Walk with the Master This Week" at the beginning of this week's material. Mark the activities you have finished by drawing vertical lines in the diamonds beside them. Finish any incomplete activities. Think about what you will say during your group session about your work on these activities.

As you complete your study of "Rely on God's Word," I hope that you realize the treasure you possess in God's Word. In the Scriptures you have everything you need to learn right doctrine and right living, to get back onto the right path, and even to reset your life course. Look to God's Word for spiritual instruction, guidance, and weapons to fight Satan. The Word will thoroughly equip you to be useful to the Master as you victoriously fend off the enemy's attacks.

DAILY MASTER COMMUNICATION GUIDE

PSALM 119:113-120

What God said to me:

Hate doublemindedness. I am sure, My word is true and sure. If you stay in my word and hold to it, you will be and you won't be double minded. My word is your shield and refuge in every situation or circumstance.

What I said to God:

Thank you O god for your sure word. Thank you for your word that never changes. Thank you for the peace in knowing that your word has been and will always be the same. Thank you for your word as my refuge and shield in times of trouble.

WEEK 4

Pray in Faith

This Week's Goal

You will be able to experience God's victory in spiritual battles by praying in faith.

My Walk with the Master This Week

You will complete the following activities to develop the six biblical disciplines. When you have completed each activity, draw a vertical line in the diamond beside it.

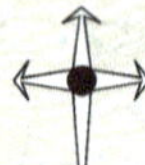

SPEND TIME WITH THE MASTER

◇ Have a quiet time each day. Check each day you have a quiet time: ❑ Sunday ❑ Monday ❑ Tuesday ❑ Wednesday ❑ Thursday ❑ Friday ❑ Saturday

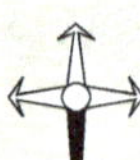

LIVE IN THE WORD

◇ Read your Bible every day. Write what God says to you and what you say to God.
◇ Memorize 1 John 5:14-15.
◇ Review 1 John 4:4, 2 Timothy 3:16-17, and Psalm 1:2-3.
◇ Meditate on 1 John 5:14-15, following "How to Use the Guide to Meditation."
◇ Continue learning the God's Word in Your Heart and Hand presentation.

PRAY IN FAITH

◇ Use the Praying in Faith form in your prayer time.

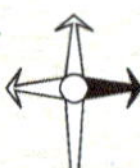

FELLOWSHIP WITH BELIEVERS

◇ Share with someone the Shield of Faith part of the Spiritual Armor.

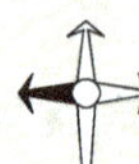

WITNESS TO THE WORLD

◇ Add to the Relational-Witnessing Chart the names of lost persons.
◇ Look for opportunities to use a witnessing booklet or a gospel presentation to share the good news with someone.

MINISTER TO OTHERS

◇ Learn the Shield of Faith part of the Spiritual Armor.

This Week's Scripture-Memory Verses

"This is the confidence we have approaching God: that if we ask anything according to his will, he hears us. And if we know that he hears us—whatever we ask—we know that we have what we asked of him" (1 John 5:14-15).

DAY 1

Claiming God's Promises

How do you let God tell you what He is doing so that you can join Him in His work? Several years ago our work group at our denominational publishing house went on a retreat to plan the products and services we would develop. The first day we shared what God had been saying to us through our daily quiet times. As we prayed, we asked the question "Lord, what are You doing or going to do that we need to be involved in?" God led us to Isaiah 61, which is quoted in Luke 4:18-19 in the margin.

We left the retreat believing that God wanted us to focus our work on the types of people Jesus came to serve: prisoners, the blind, and the oppressed. We planned products to help them. Based on this Word from the Father, we also began to look for where God was at work.

The first time I noticed God using this Scripture to lead us was when Don Dennis, a former convict, requested help in launching a program to use *MasterLife* in Texas prisons. We responded, and throughout the years thousands of prisoners have been spiritually released through *MasterLife* in the United States and in many other countries.

Then First Baptist Church of Houston offered to let us publish *First Place: A Christ-Centered Health Program.* It has helped thousands learn healthful eating and exercise habits in the context of Christian discipleship. Next Rapha, a nationally known Christian health-care organization, offered to let us publish biblical materials they had developed to help people with addictions and other emotional difficulties. We launched the LIFE Support series, which support-group ministries could use to help people with critical issues in their lives, such as painful pasts, sexual abuse, eating disorders, chemical dependency, divorce, loss, and harmful compulsions. Through these materials thousands of people have experienced healing that has brought them to Christ or has removed barriers to serving Him.

"The Spirit of the Lord
is on me,
because he hath anointed
me to preach good news
to the poor.
He has sent me to proclaim
freedom for the prisoners
and recovery of sight
for the blind,
to release the oppressed,
to proclaim the year
of the Lord's favor"
(Luke 4:18-19).

Check the answer that best describes how we approached our search for God's will for our work. We—

- ❑ **told God what we wanted to do and asked Him to bless it;**
- ❑ **implemented our ideas without praying and relied on instinct;**
- ❑ **told God what we wanted to do and asked Him to show us a Scripture that would support our strategy;**
- ☑ **asked God to show us where He wanted us to work next, and He led us to a Scripture that guided us.**

We would have been operating outside God's will if we had asked Him to bless a set of plans we had developed without consulting Him first. We asked God to show us in His Word where He wanted us to work, and He led us to a Scripture. The last answer is the correct one.

A LAMP TO YOUR FEET

God provides daily guidance for you in making decisions, facing problems, and meeting needs. As He works through the indwelling presence of the Holy Spirit, God's Word becomes active, alive, and dynamic in directing your life. As you base your life on the Word by faith, it becomes a lamp to your feet and a light for your path. In the margin read Psalm 119:105.

"Your word is a lamp to my feet and a light for my path" (Ps. 119:105).

God reveals His will through His Word to spiritually sensitive, believing Christians who meet His conditions. This week you will learn steps for praying in faith. At the end of this week's study you will be able to—

- identify occasions when you have linked prayer and God's Word;
- list three stages in making a covenant with God;
- list six steps for praying in faith;
- give examples of persons who prayed in faith on the basis of a Word from God;
- select a problem or a need about which you want to pray in faith.

A COVENANT WITH GOD

God reveals His will through His Word to spiritually sensitive, believing Christians who meet His conditions.

The relationship between praying in faith and living in the Word may have come into clearer focus as you reflected on what you have already studied in *MasterLife*. When you used the Prayer-Covenant List, you may have wondered how to find a Bible promise on which to base your prayers. A covenant is a promise or a pledge between persons to do something together, based on a common agreement. God's covenant with His people is one of the basic ideas in the Bible. Biblical covenants between God and His people had three stages:

Stage 1: God revealed His will and made a promise.
Stage 2: The people met the conditions God established.
Stage 3: The people believed God and received the blessing.

Keeping the three stages of covenant making in mind, read the following Scriptures. Circle the parts that illustrate stage 1. Underline the parts that illustrate stage 2. Use brackets for the parts that illustrate stage 3.

"I am going to bring floodwaters on the earth to destroy all life under the heavens, every creature that has the breath of life in it. Everything on earth will perish. But I will establish my covenant with you, and you will enter the ark—you and your sons and your wife and your sons' wives with you. Noah did everything just as God commanded him. Noah was six hundred years old when the floodwaters came on the earth. And Noah and his sons and his wife and his sons' wives entered the ark to escape the waters of the flood" (Gen. 6:17-18,22; 7:6-7).

"Having said this, he [Jesus] spit on the ground, made some mud with the saliva, and put it on the man's eyes. 'Go,' he told him, 'wash in the Pool of Siloam' (this word means Sent). So the man went and washed, and came home seeing" (John 9:6-7).

God made promises to His people; the people met God's conditions; they believed Him and were blessed.

Using the same stages in the process of making a covenant, beside the following accounts write the number of the first stage in which the process was not followed.

___ **1. Jim wanted to be wealthy, so he asked God to give him one million dollars.**

___ **2. As Nancy read James 1:27, the Spirit impressed her to visit a nearby orphanage, but she decided not to because she felt that it would remind her of her unhappy childhood.**

___ **3. As John heard a sermon on Matthew 28:18-20, he felt led to resign from his job and become a missionary. The next day he applied for missionary service. Soon he was offered a significant promotion at work, which he accepted.**

___ **4. Steve decided that he needed a new house, so he secured a loan and bought one.**

The answers are 1. stage 1, 2. stage 2, 3. stage 2, 4. none. This week you will learn how God reveals His will as you pray in faith.

As you learned in week 3, one way you live in the Word and the Word lives in you to help you experience victory is to think about it, or meditate on it. This week you will learn to meditate on God's Word.

Meditation has been called reflective thinking with a view to application. It involves musing, pondering, and thinking about God's Word in such a way that the message of the Scripture is applied to a specific need in your life. A great promise in God's Word, 1 John 5:14-15, deals with the relationship between God's blessings and meditation.

Meditation applies Scripture to a specific need in your life.

Turn to page 60 and read aloud 1 John 5:14-15 to begin memorizing this week's Scripture-memory verses.

"How to Use the Guide to Meditation," which follows, directs you through a process for meditating on a passage of Scripture. Use 1 John 5:14-15 and a copy of the Guide to Meditation form on page 136 in your quiet time every day this week. You do not need to finish your meditation of these verses today but may do so at your own pace between now and the end of day 5. These periods of meditation will replace your Daily Master Communication Guides this week. Copy the Guide to Meditation form for future periods of meditation.

Do a meditation study in sections a few minutes each day, concentrating on one verse a week.

HOW TO USE THE GUIDE TO MEDITATION[1]

You may do a meditation study in sections a few minutes each day, concentrating on one verse a week. Ordinarily, you may prefer to select a verse you have been memorizing or perhaps the key verse in a passage or a chapter you have read or studied during *MasterLife*. After you select a verse, pray, claiming James 1:5 for wisdom to apply God's Word.

Perimeter of the Verse
Read the verses before and after the verse to establish the theme and the setting, which will aid you in interpretation. Then write a summary of the passage.

Paraphrase the Verse
Write the verse in your own words. Say your paraphrase aloud.

Pulverize the Verse
Digest the verse by using three ways to assimilate its truths.

1. Emphasize a different word in the verse as you read or repeat it. Then state the opposite meaning to reveal what the verse says.
2. Write at least two important words from those you have emphasized in the verse.
3. Ask these questions about the two words to relate the Scripture to your needs: What? Why? When? Where? Who? How?

Let the Holy Spirit apply the verse to a need, a challenge, an opportunity, or a failure in your life.

Personalize the Verse
Let the Holy Spirit apply the verse to a need, a challenge, an opportunity, or a failure in your life. What will you *do* about this verse as it relates to your life? Be specific.

Pray the Verse Back to God
Pray the verse back to God, making it personal. Vocalize or write the verse as you pray it back to God.

Parallel Passages
Refer to other passages that emphasize the truth of the verse.

Problems in the Verse
List thoughts or ideas you might not understand or might have difficulty applying in your life. Discuss them with a Sunday School teacher or with a Christian friend.

Possibilities for Helping Others Through the Verse
Write a way you can use the verse to help another person.

Protracted Study
Record plans for further study of this verse.

DEMOLISHING PERSONAL SPIRITUAL STRONGHOLDS

By now you should be becoming more and more aware of personal spiritual strongholds in your life that need to be demolished. Based on your study in previous weeks, I hope that you are able to see changes in the areas of bitterness, speech, and lust through the work of the Holy Spirit in your life. Today you will look at another area to demolish: the stronghold of religious ritual. Four criteria in Matthew 23:1-8 tell us when religious ritual becomes a spiritual stronghold:

1. When you tell others to do what you are not practicing (vv. 2-3)
2. When you demand actions that Jesus has not commanded (v. 4)
3. When you do religious activities to be seen by others (vv. 5-7)
4. When you accept honor, position, or authority for religious service (vv. 8-12)

"Be careful not to do your 'acts of righteousness' before men, to be seen by them. If you do, you will have no reward from your Father in heaven. So when you give to the needy, do not announce it with trumpets, as the hypocrites do in the synagogues and on the streets, to be honored by men. I tell you the truth, they have received their reward in full. But when you give to the needy, do not let your left hand know what your right hand is doing, so that your giving may be in secret. Then your Father, who sees what is done in secret, will reward you. And when you pray, do not be like the hypocrites, for they love to pray standing in the synagogues and on the street corners to be seen by men. I tell you the truth, they have received their reward in full. But when you pray, go into your room, close the door and pray to your Father, who is unseen. Then your Father, who sees what is done in secret, will reward you. And when you pray, do not keep on babbling like pagans, for they think they will be heard because of their many words. Do not be like them, for your Father knows what you need before you ask him" (Matt. 6:1-8).

Read the verses in the margin, which deal with the stronghold of religious ritual. Then describe the area of religious ritual in your life that needs to be demolished, what you need to do to demolish it, and the spiritual weapon(s) to be used in demolishing it. Later this week you will record your progress.

Here is an example.

Stronghold to be demolished: teaching a Sunday School class so that others will think I am a good Christian, not from obedience to God

What I need to do to demolish it: ask God to change my heart and to help me respond to what He wants me to do

Spiritual weapons to be used: Breastplate of Righteousness—confess my sin and self-righteousness and claim the righteousness of Christ; Belt of Truth—remember that Satan tries to deceive me into believing that my worth is based on what others think. Hold to God's truth, which assures me that my worth originates in Him.

Now you try it.

Stronghold to be demolished: Using certain words in prayer aloud to show that I have a relationship with God

What I need to do to demolish it: Ask God to speak to me when I pray so that His words will be spoken, not mine

Spiritual weapon(s) to be used: Belt of Truth - remember that Satan tries to deceive me into believing that my worth is based on what others think. Hold on to God's truth, which assures me that my worth originates in Him.

DAY 2

God Communicates Truth

My longtime colleague, Jimmy Crowe, once told me about praying in faith as he prepared to undergo his third heart surgery. His two previous heart surgeries had been successful, but they occurred when Jimmy was younger. Now retired, Jimmy said he began to fear that his age—and his seeming lack of purpose as a retiree—would keep him from full recovery from another operation.

Jimmy prayed: "Lord, You know that I am much older now. My life's work is finished. Those other times You had work for me to do. Can I really endure this surgery? And should I even try now that I don't accomplish for You as much as I once did?" A friend alerted me about Jimmy's state of mind. I called him and encouraged him to help with this edition of *MasterLife* you are studying. He also received phone calls of support from friends as far away as Australia.

The night before his surgery Jimmy read from Psalms. In Psalm 118:17 the Lord revealed the answer:

> *I will not die but live,*
> *and will proclaim what the Lord has done.*

"It was a promise but also a correction," Jimmy recalled. "It was as if the Father were saying to me: 'You seem to have forgotten your primary task. You still have much to do because I have commanded that you continue to tell of Me and My love for people.' Afterward the doctor said that this surgery was easy, and my recovery was quick. The time since then has been one of the most fruitful periods of my ministry, with many opportunities to teach and minister."

"Continue to tell of Me and My love for people."

Describe a crisis when you found comfort and victory from Scripture.

I felt like I was losing my mind and I turned to Phillippians 4.

You may think, *I'd really like to pray in faith, based on a Word from the Lord, but how can I do that? How can I know that God is speaking to me through a specific part of His Word to apply to a specific situation? How can I use promises from His Word to help me claim victory in spiritual warfare?* When you act in faith on what God communicates to you as truth, you will have victory.

When you act in faith on what God communicates to you as truth, you will have victory.

This week you will discover six steps for praying in faith. The first three relate to God's communicating truth to you. The second three relate to your communicating faith to God. Today you will explore the first step.

GOD COMMUNICATES TRUTH TO YOU
1. Abide in Christ.
2. Abide in the Word.
3. Allow the Holy Spirit to lead you in truth.

Your greatest concern as a Christian disciple is to find and do God's will. How do you find God's will? Jesus no longer physically walks by and beckons you to follow Him. Yet He is just as concerned about your doing His will. He has given you the written Word of God, which He reveals to you through the Holy Spirit. He gives you light through His Word, and He expects you to follow it by faith. God "works in you to will and to act according to his good purpose" (Phil. 2:13).

Your greatest concern as a Christian disciple is to find and do God's will.

Praying in faith is two-way communication: God reveals truth to you, and you exercise faith toward Him. The Praying in Faith form (p. 139) provides a practical checklist to help you apply this teaching.

This is the confidence we have approaching God. That if we ask anything according to His will, He hears us. And if He hears us whatever we ask we know that we have what we ask of Him. 1 John 5:14-15

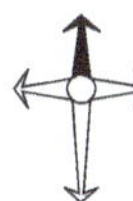

"Guide to Praying in Faith," which follows, uses elements of the Praying in Faith form (p. 139) to help you work through a problem you currently face. Use copies of the Praying in Faith form to pray about future problems.

STEP 1: ABIDE IN CHRIST

GUIDE TO PRAYING IN FAITH

What is the problem? Achieving success and feeling like it is taking too long for me to get there.

First, recognize that God can and will work in your problem for your good and for His glory. Romans 8:28 reminds you, "We know that in all things God works for the good of those who love him, who have been called according to his purpose." That does not mean that all things *are* good but that ultimately, God will work together all things to produce good.

Second, recognize that God is sovereign. He knew about your circumstances before they happened. Although God may not have caused the events to occur, He did not choose to alter their course.

Recognize that God can and will work in your problem for your good and for His glory.

How could God possibly use my problem?
- ☒ **A platform for God to demonstrate His power**
- ☒ **A blessing from God for which I have not asked**
- ☒ **An opportunity for God to develop in me faith, love, patience, or another Christlike character trait**

☒ **An opportunity to develop a more effective prayer life**

Rewrite the problem in the form of a question to God.

God, is it your will for me to have the things that I asked, in terms of my success?

Am I abiding in Christ and committed to His will for my life?
☒ **Yes** ❑ **No**

"If you remain in me and my words remain in you, ask whatever you wish, and it will be given you" (John 15:7).

The first way to learn God's will is to abide, or remain, in Christ, as John 15:7 reminds you. Read this verse in the margin.

What does *remaining in Christ* mean to you?

Allowing God to be your savior and maintaining the relationship you have with Him.

Are you living in vital connection with Christ, the Vine? ☒ **Yes** ❑ **No If not, what do you need to do to be in a right relationship with Him?**

____

Be sure that your fleshly desires are not standing in the way of your discovering God's will.

Make sure that you are abiding in Christ. Lay aside your own will and desires, as much as possible, to seek God's will. Be sure that your fleshly desires are not standing in the way of your discovering God's will. These are the areas that can be affected:

❑ Your senses (body)
☒ Your logic (mind)
☒ Your feelings (emotions)
☒ Your wishes (will)
☒ Your desires (flesh)

In the list above, check any areas that might be keeping you from discovering God's will.

Stop and ask for the Holy Spirit to fill you and to lead you to know and do God's will as you abide in Him.

This is the confidence we have in approaching God, that if we ask anything according to His will, He hears us. And if we know He hears us, whatever we ask we know that we have what we ask of Him. 1 John 5:14-15

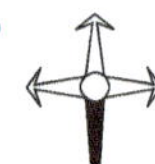

This week's Scripture-memory verses, 1 John 5:14-15, remind you to accept God's Word in faith. Try to write these verses from memory in the margin.

Meditate on 1 John 5:14-15 during your quiet time today, following the guidance on page 64.

DAY 3

Turning to God First

Today you will continue to examine six steps for praying in faith. The first three relate to discovering God's will about a matter. Yesterday you learned the first one. Today you will examine the second.

GOD COMMUNICATES TRUTH TO YOU
1. Abide in Christ.
2. Abide in the Word.
3. Allow the Holy Spirit to lead you in truth.

STEP 2: ABIDE IN THE WORD

In John 15:7 a second step to learning God's will about a matter is abiding in the Word. When you have a problem, first turn to God and seek His Word to find the solution to your problem. Read Psalm 27:13-14 in the margin.

"I am still confident of this:
I will see the goodness
of the Lord
in the land of the living.
Wait for the Lord;
be strong and take heart
and wait for the Lord"
(Ps. 27:13-14).

"Guide to Praying in Faith," which follows, uses elements of the Praying in Faith form (p. 139) to help you continue working through the problem you identified in day 2. Use copies of the Praying in Faith form to pray about future problems.

GUIDE TO PRAYING IN FAITH
Ask yourself:
- **Have I brought my problem to God first?** ❑ Yes ❑ No
- **Am I systematically abiding in His Word?** ❑ Yes ❑ No
- **Am I willing to wait for His solution?** ❑ Yes ❑ No

To whom have you already gone to get help in solving your problem? Check all that apply.

❑ **neighbor**	❑ **counselor**
❑ **physician**	❑ **relative**
❑ **lawyer**	❑ **fellow church member**
❑ **accountant**	☒ **other:** Friend

Sometimes you consult neighbors, doctors, lawyers, accountants, counselors, or others instead of God. God uses other sources to help you solve your problem, but He wants you to seek Him first.

Read the Scriptures in the margin on the following page and write in your own words what each teaches about how to abide, or remain, in the Word.

"If you hold to my teaching, you are really my disciples. Then you will know the truth, and the truth will set you free" (John 8:31).

"Whoever has my commands and obeys them, he is the one who loves me. He who loves me will be loved by my Father, and I too will love him and show myself to him" (John 14:21).

"He knows the way that I take;
when he has tested me,
I will come forth as gold.
My feet have closely followed his steps;
I have kept to his way
without turning aside.
I have not departed from
the commands of his lips;
I have treasured the words
of his mouth more than my
daily bread" (Job 23:10-12).

John 8:31: Stay in the word, then you will know the truth and because you know the truth, you will be free.

John 14:21: If you stay in the word and obey them that shows your love for Jesus and if you love Jesus then you're loved by God. You will also be loved by Jesus if you stay in the word and obey them.

Job 23:10-12: When you stay in the word you will past any test or trial that comes your way. The word should be to you as your daily meal.

Write *A* beside the accounts describing persons who are abiding properly in the Word.

A **Oscar is studying the Bible and doing God's will as best he knows how. Whenever he fails, he asks for forgiveness. He is committed to doing whatever God asks him to do.**

___ **Reggie is active in his church but does not see how the Bible relates to what he does every day. He reads some of it every week. He has many goals for his life. He has asked God to help him achieve them and believes that God will.**

A **Stella has discovered several verses that apply to her life as she reads the Bible day by day. She has underlined the conditions in each verse and is doing as commanded.**

A **Richard believes that God gave him a promise through a verse he memorized. But it has been six months, and little has happened. He believes that God gives more light to those who follow the light they have. So he keeps obeying the Word and believes that he will receive more light in God's time.**

As you meet the conditions for learning God's will about a matter, you can receive input on what God's will is for your life and prayers. In the exercise all of the individuals are abiding properly in the Word except Reggie, who was not discerning God's will through the Word.

What are ways to let God speak to you as you abide in His Word?

- Read the Bible systematically and let God speak through passages He brings to mind.
- Look for specific principles and truths that apply to your situation.
- Look for the meaning of the Scripture passage to the original readers.
- Look for a present-day application of a truth or a biblical situation.
- Be willing to look and wait for a Word from God.

You may be concerned when I suggest that you find a specific verse to communicate in a present-day situation. You might think, *Certainly you don't mean that I should open the Bible and put my finger on a verse at random.* Many abuses of Scripture occur when people use that approach. Clearly, this is not what is meant by praying in faith by claiming a verse from God's Word. It is not a verse you grab but a verse that grabs you as the Holy Spirit applies it to you in your context.

Read James 4:3 in the margin. Why was this prayer not answered?

Asked with wrong motives, motives not of God.

"When you ask, you do not receive, because you ask with wrong motives, that you may spend what you get on your pleasures" (Jas. 4:3).

Abuses of Scripture can also occur when you pray with wrong motives. The person to whom James 4:3 referred prayed according to the flesh rather than abiding in Christ.

Ask yourself these questions again about your problem:

- **Have I brought my problem to God first?** ☒ **Yes** ❑ **No**
- **Am I systematically abiding in His Word?** ☒ **Yes** ❑ **No**
- **Am I willing to wait for His solution?** ☒ **Yes** ❑ **No**

If you cannot answer yes to these questions, go back to step 1 and work through these matters before you continue.

Write the first two steps for praying in faith that you have studied before you study the third one tomorrow.

1. Abide in Christ.
2. Abide in the word.
3. Allow the Holy Spirit to lead you in all truth.

PUTTING ON THE SPIRITUAL ARMOR

This week you will study the Shield of Faith as you continue to learn the Spiritual Armor. Turn to pages 129–31 and quickly review the entire Spiritual Armor presentation, with special emphasis on the Shield of Faith. By the end of this study you will be able to explain the entire presentation in your own words.

In one hand you hold the Sword of the Spirit. In the other hand picture yourself holding the Shield of Faith. The Roman shield was a long, oblong piece of wood. When the enemy's fiery arrows hit it, they buried themselves in the wood and were extinguished. So as the arrows of evil are aimed at you, advance with the Shield of Faith and quench the fiery darts of the wicked. Let the Shield of Faith remind you to do the following.

Advance with the Shield of Faith and quench the fiery darts of the wicked.

1. Claim the victory. Faith is the victory that overcomes the world (see 1 John 5:4).
2. Advance in faith. Faith without works is dead (see Jas. 2:20). Put feet to your prayers.
3. Quench all of the fiery darts of the wicked.

Focus on the first of the three reminders. Claim the fact that you already have the victory. As you pray, thank God in advance because you know that you will be victorious.

Practice saying this week's Scripture-memory verses, 1 John 5:14-15, to a friend or a family member. Explain what these verses are helping you learn about praying in faith.

Meditate on 1 John 5:14-15 during your quiet time today, following the guidance on page 64.

DAY 4

Leading You in Truth

Today you will continue to examine six steps for praying in faith. The first three relate to discovering God's will about a matter. You have learned the first two. Today you will examine the third.

GOD COMMUNICATES TRUTH TO YOU
1. Abide in Christ.
2. Abide in the Word.
3. **Allow the Holy Spirit to lead you in truth.**

STEP 3: ALLOW THE HOLY SPIRIT TO LEAD YOU IN TRUTH

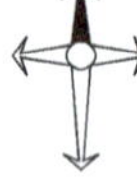

"Guide to Praying in Faith," which follows, uses elements of the Praying in Faith form (p. 139) to help you continue working through the problem you identified in day 2. Use copies of the Praying in Faith form to pray about future problems.

GUIDE TO PRAYING IN FAITH
Am I allowing the Holy Spirit to fill me, to lead me to a Scripture, and to apply it to my problem? ☒ **Yes** ☐ **No**
What is the Scripture?

1 John 5:14-15

How do I think this Scripture applies to my problem?

I need to have more confidence that god hears me and if I believe, I will what I ask of Him.

God reveals His will through His Word but only to those who allow the Holy Spirit to lead them in truth.

God reveals His will through His Word but only to those who allow the Holy Spirit to lead them in truth. The Holy Spirit needs to work both to reveal God's truth to you and to help you receive the truth.

Read the Scriptures in the margin. What is one of the basic jobs of the Holy Spirit?

Guide us into truth.

Notice that in John 16:13-15 Jesus promised in three different ways that the Spirit will reveal truth to you. Underline them.

"When he, the Spirit of truth, comes he will guide you into all truth. He will not speak on his own; he will speak only what he hears, and he will tell you what is yet to come. He will bring glory to me by taking from what is mine and making it known to you. All that belongs to the Father is mine. That is why I said the Spirit will take from what is mine and make it known to you" (John 16:13-15).

"The Counselor, the Holy Spirit, whom the Father will send in my name, will teach you all things and will remind you of everything I have said to you" (John 14:26).

The Holy Spirit is the teacher in Christians' lives. Under His guidance the words of the Bible become a Word from the Father for each of us. He is present as each Christian studies. You may have underlined that the Spirit "will guide you," "will speak," and "will tell you" to indicate how the Holy Spirit works.

A basic job of the Holy Spirit is to show truth to you. If you read the Bible with a logical, analytical approach and conclude, *This is what God is saying to me*, you are missing the vital element of letting the Spirit guide you and illuminate the Scripture. When you let the Spirit do so, you can then walk on the basis of that illumination. You might think, *That approach sounds a little mystical to me.* The essence of true Christianity *is* a little mystical. It is your relationship with Jesus Christ. You cannot put it in a test tube. The Holy Spirit reveals God's presence in your life. The Holy Spirit inspired those who wrote the Word. Now the Holy Spirit works in you to interpret what is written and to help you apply it to your life.

Continue reading and studying until the Holy Spirit impresses you with a Scripture. As the Holy Spirit illuminates the Scripture and you apply it to your situation, ask these test questions about the conclusion you have drawn:

- Is it consistent with truth revealed in the rest of the Bible?
- Is it consistent with God's character?
- Is it consistent with the meaning of the Scripture in context?
- Does it violate the original meaning of the Scripture?
- Does the Holy Spirit continue to bear witness to its validity as you continue to pray about it?

Review by listing the three ways to get input from God on which to base your prayers of faith. Remember that these are the first three of the six steps for praying in faith.

God communicates truth to you when you—

1. A bide in Christ

2. A bide in the word

3. A llow the Holy Spirit to lead you in truth

A systematic study of God's Word and a systematic application of His Word in your life by the Holy Spirit help prevent abuses of praying in faith. Write yes beside the following situations in which

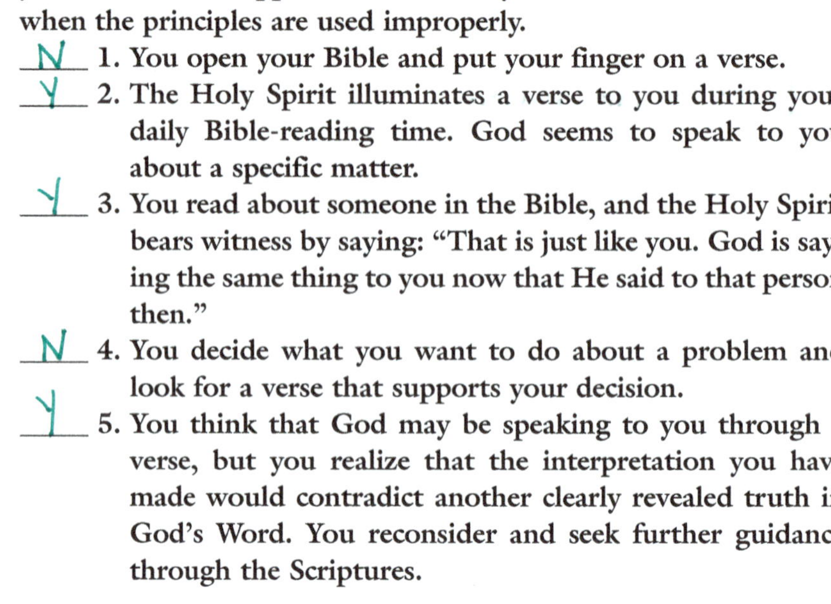

you see a correct application of what you have studied. Write no when the principles are used improperly.

N **1. You open your Bible and put your finger on a verse.**

Y **2. The Holy Spirit illuminates a verse to you during your daily Bible-reading time. God seems to speak to you about a specific matter.**

Y **3. You read about someone in the Bible, and the Holy Spirit bears witness by saying: "That is just like you. God is saying the same thing to you now that He said to that person then."**

N **4. You decide what you want to do about a problem and look for a verse that supports your decision.**

Y **5. You think that God may be speaking to you through a verse, but you realize that the interpretation you have made would contradict another clearly revealed truth in God's Word. You reconsider and seek further guidance through the Scriptures.**

Although some cases certainly exist in which God has used the method of turning to a verse to which your Bible opens, God usually does not speak to you when you randomly select a passage or when you make a decision about a matter before you seek His counsel. He speaks to you when the Holy Spirit illuminates a verse for you during your regular Bible reading or when the Spirit tells you that your situation is like the one you are reading about. If you are in doubt or think that another Scripture contradicts the premise of your passage, seek further guidance in the Word. Situations 2, 3, and 5 are the ones in which the principles you have studied are applied properly.

What if you do not find a Scripture that gives you direct guidance for a problem or a need? Continue reading your Bible and praying until an answer comes (see Matt. 7:7-8). God may be letting you come to the end of yourself before He reveals His answer. Wait on the Lord. What if you must make a decision before you get an answer? Be sure that it must immediately be made before using your own reason (see Prov. 3: 5-6; 16:3). But if circumstances force you to make a decision before you get a specific Word from God, submit yourself to His will and make the decision in light of the total biblical revelation and the Spirit's leading.

The Holy Spirit illuminates the Word for those who seek to know and do God's will.

The Holy Spirit illuminates the Word for those who seek to know and do God's will. You discover God's will through the systematic intake of the Word. It becomes God's personal Word to you as you obey it by faith.

PUTTING ON THE SPIRITUAL ARMOR

In day 3 you reviewed the importance of the Shield of Faith as you continued to learn the Spiritual Armor presentation. You learned three steps for putting on the Shield of Faith. Review them on page 71.

Focus on the second step in putting on the Shield of Faith. If God has given you a Word, claim the victory and advance in faith. Ask Him to give you courage to move forward boldly as the Lord directs you and not just to give lip-service to your faith.

If God has given you a Word, claim the victory and advance in faith.

GOD'S WORD IN YOUR HEART AND HAND

Last week you began learning a simple illustration for grasping the Sword of the Spirit, God's Word, so that you can live in victory. This week you will learn scriptural support for the illustration.

Referring to the hand drawing on page 132, review the Scripture references in "Level 2: Explanation" (p. 133) in the God's Word in Your Heart and Hand presentation.

On the illustration below write the five ways to get God's Word into your heart and the way to get a firm grip on the Word. Then add the following Scripture references in the appropriate places on the drawing. Refer to pages 132–34 if you need to review.

- **Mark 4:23; Romans 10:17**
- **Psalm 1:2-3; Joshua 1:8**
- **Revelation 1:3**
- **Acts 17:11; 2 Timothy 2:15**
- **Psalm 119:9,11; Deuteronomy 6:6**
- **Luke 6:46-49; James 1:22**

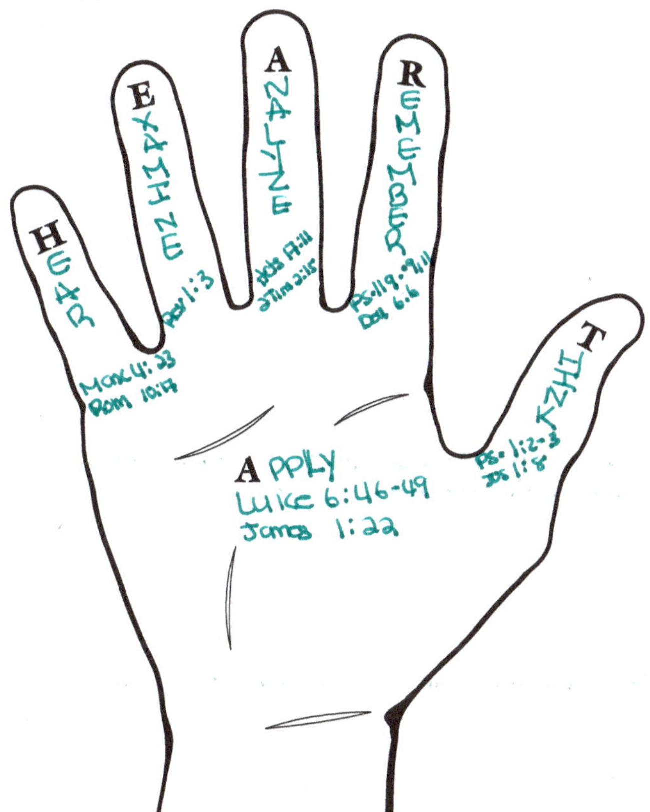

Meditate on 1 John 5:14-15 during your quiet time today, following the guidance on page 64. Then test your memorization by trying to say these verses aloud. Recall from memory your Scripture-memory verses from weeks 1–3.

DAY 5

Communicating Your Faith

This week you are learning six steps for praying in faith. The first three relate to God's communicating truth to you. The last three relate to your communicating faith to God:

> **YOU COMMUNICATE FAITH TO GOD**
> **4. Ask according to God's will.**
> 5. Accept God's will in faith.
> 6. Act on the basis of God's Word to you.
> These last three steps can be accomplished only after God has led you to know His will through the Word.

"If you remain in me and my words remain in you, ask whatever you wish, and it will be given to you" (John 15:7).

"Ask and it will be given to you; seek and you will find; knock and the door will be opened to you. For everyone who asks receives; he who seeks finds; and to him who knocks, the door will be opened" (Matt. 7:7-8).

"You want something but don't get it. You kill and covet, but you cannot have what you want. You quarrel and fight. You do not have, because you do not ask God. When you ask, you do not receive, because you ask with wrong motives, that you may spend what you get on your pleasures" (Jas. 4:2-3).

STEP 4: ASK ACCORDING TO GOD'S WILL

"Guide to Praying in Faith," which follows, uses elements of the Praying in Faith form (p. 139) to help you continue working on the problem you identified in day 2. If you do not have God's leading yet about the problem you have been praying about, review the material you have studied and wait to complete the questions about your request until you have a Scripture on which to base your faith. Use copies of the Praying in Faith form to pray about future problems.

> **GUIDE TO PRAYING IN FAITH**
> **What is my specific request?**
>
> I want to be able to take care of my mom in a financial way.

Read John 15:7 and Matthew 7:7-8 in the margin. What is the additional step you must take after God has revealed His will about a particular matter through His Word?

Ask and it will be given to you

Read James 4:2-3 in the margin. On the next page write two reasons many people do not have all God wants to give them.

① Do not ask God for what they want

① Ask with the wrong motives

God is willing to give to us abundantly, but we often fail to ask for the things He wants us to have. He expects us to ask after we discern what His will is for us. When we do not ask or when we ask with improper motives, we do not receive the good gifts God has for us.

Many incidents in the Bible illustrate occasions when persons discerned God's will and then asked on the basis of it. When Nehemiah learned about his people in exile, he remembered the word of God to Moses (see Neh. 1:8-9). On the basis of that, Nehemiah prayed that God would allow him to go back to Jerusalem and build the walls. Read Nehemiah's words in the margin. The crippled man Jesus healed at the pool of Bethesda had lain there for 38 years, but then Jesus told him, "Pick up your mat and walk." Read John 5:5-9 in the margin. On the basis of that word from Jesus, he stood and walked.

"Remember the instruction you gave your servant Moses, saying, 'If you are unfaithful, I will scatter you among the nations, but if you return to me and obey my commands, then even if your exiled people are at the farthest horizon, I will gather them from there and bring them to the place I have chosen as a dwelling for my Name' " (Neh. 1:8-9).

"One who was there had been an invalid for thirty-eight years. When Jesus saw him lying there and learned that he had been in this condition for a long time, he asked him, 'Do you want to get well?' 'Sir,' the invalid replied, 'I have no one to help me into the pool when the water is stirred. While I am trying to get in, someone else goes down ahead of me.' Then Jesus said to him, 'Get up! Pick up your mat and walk.' At once the man was cured; he picked up his mat and walked" (John 5:5-9).

Describe a time when God showed you His will through Scripture.

Acts 17:27 [When I am feeling lost, like I should not be in a place that I am. I am encouraged by this word.

God will do as He has promised or will help you do as He has directed you. The first step in communicating your faith to God is to ask according to His will. God's greatest blessings and your greatest usefulness in His kingdom result when you completely fulfill His covenant.

Remain in the verse God reveals to you. As you read your Bible each day, God's Spirit has the power to make His will known to you. Ask God to answer, based on His Word, and be specific in your request.

STEP 5: ACCEPT GOD'S WILL IN FAITH

This week's Scripture-memory verses, 1 John 5:14-15, identify another step that communicates your faith to God.

Say aloud this week's Scripture-memory verses, 1 John 5:14-15. Write the step the verses mention.

Ask according to God's will.

The second way to communicate faith is to accept God's will in faith:

YOU COMMUNICATE FAITH TO GOD

4. Ask according to God's will.
5. Accept God's will in faith.
6. Act on the basis of God's Word to you.

If God has said it, believe it and practice it. I do not always know how He will solve my problem, but I begin to accept as certainty the fact that He will provide an answer, and I praise Him for it.

"Guide to Praying in Faith," which follows, uses elements of the Praying in Faith form (p. 139) to help you continue working on the problem you identified in day 2. Use copies of the Praying in Faith form to pray about future problems.

GUIDE TO PRAYING IN FAITH

What do I believe that God will do about my problem?

He will give me what I asked for.
I believe He will use it to develop the character that he wants me to have. (Patience, Faith)

Do I accept God's promise as a God-revealed certainty?

☒ **Yes** ❑ **No**

First John 5:14-15 says that we can feel assured that if we ask according to His will, He hears us. We can depend on God's Word in this matter and can accept it not by signs but by faith. God will answer when Christians ask according to His will. When the Holy Spirit puts together truth and faith in your life, the request you make will be answered.

Praying in faith based on God's Word is not a new concept. Individuals of faith have been taking these steps since Bible times. Read the Scriptures in the margin. Daniel prayed that God's anger would be turned away from Jerusalem and the desolate sanctuary restored. He prayed because he read that Jeremiah had written that God would bring his people back from exile after 70 years. After 68 years there was no sign that God was accomplishing this. Jesus prayed that God's will would be done about the crucifixion. He knew that the Scriptures, as recorded in Isaiah, needed to be fulfilled.

Make your request specific so that you will know whether it is answered. Begin to visualize the request being granted. Live in the joy of His assurance through the Word. Memorize and repeat His Word to you. Affirm it whenever doubts arise. Trust what God has told you in His Word rather than your feelings or hopes.

Stop and pray the following prayer or one similar to it: "Father, I accept Your Word in faith. I believe that You will provide an answer for my problem, and I praise You already, even though I don't know the specific details of how You will answer. I claim this verse, 1 John 5:14-15, as Your Word to me, and I thank You for revealing Your Word to me. Amen."

STEP 6: ACT ON THE BASIS OF GOD'S WORD TO YOU

One step remains in communicating your faith to God:

"In the first year of his reign, I, Daniel, understood from the Scriptures, according to the word of the Lord given to Jeremiah the prophet, that the desolation of Jerusalem would last seventy years. So I turned to the Lord God and pleaded with him in prayer and petition, in fasting, and in sackcloth and ashes. 'O Lord, in keeping with all your righteous acts, turn away your anger and your wrath from Jerusalem, your city, your holy hill. Our sins and the iniquities of our fathers have made Jerusalem and your people an object of scorn to all those around us. Now, our God, hear the prayers and petitions of your servant. For your sake, O Lord, look with favor on your desolate sanctuary'" (Dan. 9:2-3,16-17).

"Then he said to them, 'My soul is overwhelmed with sorrow to the point of death. Stay here and keep watch with me.' Going a little farther, he fell with his face to the ground and prayed, 'My Father, if it is possible, may this cup be taken from me. Yet not as I will, but as you will'" (Matt. 26:38-39).

"Do you think I cannot call on my Father, and he will at once put at my disposal more than twelve legions of angels? But how then would the Scriptures be fulfilled that say it must happen this way?" (Matt. 26:53-54).

YOU COMMUNICATE FAITH TO GOD
4. Ask according to God's will.
5. Accept God's will in faith.
6. Act on the basis of God's Word to you.

The third step to take in communicating your faith to God is to act on the basis of the Word from God. After you have prayed in faith, you act even when you cannot see the answer to your request. Too many of us want to depend on our physical senses and our intellect for truth.

Jesus often instructed persons to do something as evidence of their faith before He answered their requests. Read John 9:7 and Luke 17:14 in the margin. The essence of walking by faith is that we believe God and what He communicates through the objective Word of God with the subjective application of the Spirit of God. Then we act because we know that it is true, even when our physical senses do not say so. When you pray in faith, you begin to act as if you already know what will happen.

" 'Go,' he told him, 'Wash in the Pool of Siloam' (this word means Sent). So the man went and washed, and came home seeing" (John 9:7).

"When he saw them, he said, 'Go, show yourselves to the priests.' And as they went, they were cleansed" (Luke 17:14).

Following the guidance on page 64, meditate on this week's Scripture-memory verses, 1 John 5:14-15, as quoted in the margin from *The Amplified Bible.* This translation gives several possible meanings of selected Greek words in which the New Testament was written. Underline the words that give reasons for you to act in faith on the basis of God's Word for your need.

"This is the confidence—the assurance, the [privilege of] boldness—which we have in Him: [we are sure] that if we ask anything (make any request) according to His will (in agreement with His own plan) He listens to and hears us. And if (since) we [positively] know that He listens to us in whatever we ask, we also know [with settled and absolute knowledge] that we have [granted us as our present possessions] the request made of Him" (1 John 5:14-15, AMP).

Review your Scripture-memory verses from previous weeks.

Now you will respond to the final questions on the Praying in Faith form. As you respond, consider these suggestions.

- If the answer is obvious, write it down.
- If the answer is long in coming, be faithful in believing prayer (see Rom. 4:18-21).
- If the answer is not given in the way you asked, use the Praying in Faith form (p. 139) to repeat the process for further guidance.
- When you are convinced that God has answered the prayer differently from your request, accept it.
- Keep a record of God's answers to prayers. Watch your faith grow.

For example, God sometimes allows problems to enter our lives to increase our dependence on and faith in Him. When something like this occurs, pray, "Teach me through this so that I'll know better how to walk in the Spirit by faith."

"Guide to Praying in Faith," which follows, uses elements of the Praying in Faith form (p. 139) to help you continue working on the problem you identified in day 2. Use copies of the Praying in Faith form to pray about future problems.

GUIDE TO PRAYING IN FAITH

What actions(s) will I take, based on this Word from God?

____

____

What action(s) did God take in answer to my prayer of faith?

____

____

What else do I need to do?

____

____

You show a full faith when you act on the basis of what you believe.

Now carry out those actions. You show a full faith when you act on the basis of what you believe. God delights in answering the prayers of His faithful, believing servants. Use the same six steps with your major problems and decisions.

To review, write the six steps for praying in faith.

God communicates truth to me:

1. Abide in Christ
2. Abide in the word.
3. Allow the Holy Spirit to lead me in truth.

I communicate faith to God:

4. Ask according to His will.
5. Accept God's will in Faith.
6. Act on the basis of God's word to me.

DEMOLISHING PERSONAL SPIRITUAL STRONGHOLDS

In day 1 you identified a stronghold you wanted to demolish in the area of religious ritual. Today give a progress report on how you have used the spiritual weapon(s) you listed to demolish this stronghold.

How I have used a spiritual weapon(s) to help demolish religious ritual:

Use Matthew 6:5-13, when I pray it should be me communicating in a personal space with God, whether I am in public or not.

PUTTING ON THE SPIRITUAL ARMOR

Continue to study the importance of taking up the Shield of Faith. Review on page 71 the three steps for putting on the shield.

Focus on the third step in taking up the Shield of Faith. Stop and pray, asking God to help you hold up the Shield of Faith when Satan hurls darts at you that would cause you to doubt. Act on faith and not from fear.

Share with your family, a Christian friend, or a group the Shield of Faith part of the Spiritual Armor.

Many persons do not know the Source of faith.

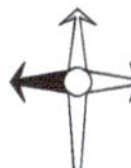

Add to the Relational-Witnessing Chart (p. 135) and to the Prayer-Covenant List (p. 143) the names of persons who do not know Christ.

Look for opportunities to use a witnessing booklet or another gospel presentation to share the gospel with someone. Here are more suggestions for doing so.

- **Ask, Would you follow along with me while I read something that has made a difference in my life?**
- **As you read, stop periodically and involve the person in what you are reading. Ask nonthreatening questions like, Have you ever had an experience like the one the book describes? or, Have you ever had questions like the ones the book describes?**
- **To hold the person's attention, ask him or her to read some verses the book mentions rather than your reading all of them.**

Look for opportunities to share the gospel with someone.

Meditate on 1 John 5:14-15 during your quiet time today, following the guidance on page 64.

List problems or requests for which you are seeking God's direction through His Word.

Interpreting dreams, obtaining financial freedom, obtain mental freedom, ways that I can share my faith that feels natural to me.

Make copies of the Praying in Faith form on page 139. Record the problems you listed and begin to pray for them as you answer the questions on the form during the next two weeks.

HAS THIS WEEK MADE A DIFFERENCE?

Review "My Walk with the Master This Week" at the beginning of this week's material. Mark the activities you have finished by drawing vertical lines in the diamonds beside them. Finish any incomplete activities. Think about what you will say during your group session about your work on these activities.

Check the following statements that describe you.

- [x] **God wants me to discern His will by staying connected to His Word.**
- [x] **God truly desires to answer my prayers that are prayed according to His will.**
- [x] **Through the Holy Spirit, God's Word becomes active and dynamic in directing my life.**
- [x] **God is interested in revealing His desires about everyday matters in my life.**
- [x] **God will show me answers to my problems when I pray in faith.**
- [x] **God will give me victory over Satan's attacks when I pray in faith.**

God is eager to give good gifts to His children who pray in faith based on His Word.

As you conclude your study of "Pray in Faith," I hope that you are digging deep into God's Word to find the precious promises that await you. I hope that now you are more aware of God's eagerness to give good gifts to His children who pray in faith based on His Word. I hope that this week's study has begun to revolutionize your prayer life and has given you encouragement about prayer so that you can live victoriously when Satan attacks.

1. Guide to Meditation steps, © Waylon Moore.

WEEK 5

Look to Jesus

This Week's Goal

You will be able to write your life purpose and life goals.

My Walk with the Master This Week

You will complete the following activities to develop the six biblical disciplines. When you have completed each activity, draw a vertical line in the diamond beside it.

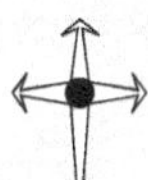

SPEND TIME WITH THE MASTER

◇ Have a quiet time each day. Check each day you have a quiet time: ❑ Sunday ❑ Monday ❑ Tuesday ❑ Wednesday ❑ Thursday ❑ Friday ❑ Saturday

LIVE IN THE WORD

◇ Read your Bible every day. Write what God says to you and what you say to God.
◇ Memorize Ephesians 6:18.
◇ Review 1 John 4:4, 2 Timothy 3:16-17, Psalm 1:2-3, and 1 John 5:14-15.
◇ Continue learning the God's Word in Your Heart and Hand presentation.

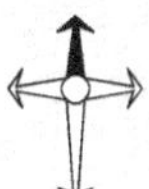

PRAY IN FAITH

◇ Use "Guide to Intercession" during your prayer time.
◇ Begin making a personal prayer journal.

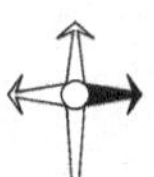

FELLOWSHIP WITH BELIEVERS

◇ Show God's love to someone every day this week.
◇ Share with someone the Gospel Shoes part of the Spiritual Armor.
◇ Select one level of the God's Word in Your Heart and Hand presentation and share it with your family or a Christian friend.

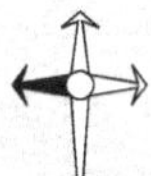

WITNESS TO THE WORLD

◇ Read "Expanding Your Witness Circle."
◇ Add to the Relational-Witnessing Chart the names of lost persons.

MINISTER TO OTHERS

◇ Learn the Gospel Shoes part of the Spiritual Armor.

This Week's Scripture-Memory Verse

"Pray in the Spirit on all occasions with all kinds of prayers and requests. With this in mind, be alert and always keep on praying for all the saints" (Eph. 6:18).

DAY 1

Your Overarching Vision

Define your life purpose and life goals so that Satan cannot distract you.

When you are at war, you need an overarching vision to stay focused on what you need to accomplish. We are in a huge battle with Satan. You must know clearly what your life purpose is if you are to be a part of God's purpose. You must define your life purpose and life goals so that in the midst of warfare Satan cannot distract you from what God wants you to do.

THE IMPORTANCE OF STAYING FOCUSED

Jesus' experience in the wilderness clarified His life purpose. He had just been baptized and had heard John pronounce Him "the Lamb of God who takes away the sin of the world" (John 1:29). His Father had said, "This is my Son, whom I love" (Matt. 3:17). In the wilderness Jesus came to grips with the fact that He had the power to do everything Satan tempted Him to do. Yet He chose to do things the Father's way instead.

You must know your life purpose when you are in the midst of battle. God uses His Word to teach you your life purpose and goals. God gave me a Scripture passage, Psalm 71:17-18, when I was in my 20s. Although I did not fully understand it, I felt that it was a goal for my life that He had given to me. The passage says:

> *O God, thou hast taught me from my youth: and hitherto have I declared thy wondrous works. Now also when I am old and greyheaded, O God, forsake me not; until I have shewed thy strength unto this generation, and thy power to every one that is to come (KJV).*

I claimed those verses for the rest of my life, asking the Lord not to forsake me until I had shown His strength to this generation and His power to future generations. I did not know what that meant then as the pastor of a small church while in seminary, and I still do not understand all it means. But those verses have focused my life on glorifying God so that people now and in future generations may know Him. From the day after I was saved as a child, I have told people what God did to save me. This has been a mark in my ministry—to tell others about the wonderful things God does.

A Christian's purpose and goals must be Christ-centered.

Someone who aims at nothing usually hits it. As the Bible says, "Where there is no vision, the people perish" (Prov. 29:18, KJV). Great accomplishments can be traced to people with a vision, or a life purpose. A Christian's purpose and goals must be Christ-centered.

Your study this week will help you determine your life purpose and set life goals consistent with the plan God wishes to accomplish in spite of spiritual warfare. At the end of this week's study you will be able to—

- define *life purpose* and *life goals* and explain the difference;
- identify Christ's life purpose and life goals;
- write your life purpose and life goals;
- prioritize your life goals;
- commit yourself to accomplishing your life goals in spite of Satan's opposition.

DISCOVERING YOUR LIFE PURPOSE

One blessing of being a Christian is having a purpose for living. Without Christ, life resembles a jigsaw puzzle. The pieces do not fit together when we have no vision of the finished product. A believer's completed life vision should come from God and should resemble Christ Himself. In Him we discover the meaning of our lives.

Read John 4:31-34 in the margin. What did Jesus say was His purpose for living?

"His disciples urged him, 'Rabbi, eat something.' But he said to them, 'I have food to eat that you know nothing about.' Then his disciples said to each other, 'Could someone have brought him food?' 'My food,' said Jesus, 'is to do the will of him who sent me and to finish his work' " (John 4:31-34).

To do the will of him who sent me and to finish his work.

Jesus did the Father's work in complete obedience. Nothing was as important to Him as doing God's will and finishing the work He was sent to do.

> A life purpose is an overarching goal for you to accomplish in your lifetime. It provides direction for everyday activities and determines your priorities.

Some people spend their lives trying to be successful. Others desire wealth or fame. Others vainly attempt to find happiness, love, and security through human relationships. The Westminster Confession states that humans' chief end is to glorify God and to enjoy Him forever.

A scribe asked Jesus to summarize humanity's duty. In His reply Jesus called attention to two life purposes.

Read Mark 12:29-31 in the margin and underline the two life purposes Jesus identified.

" 'The most important one,' answered Jesus, 'is this: "Hear, O Israel, the Lord our God, the Lord is one. Love the Lord your God with all your heart and with all your soul and with all your mind and with all your strength." The second is this: "Love your neighbor as yourself." There is no commandment greater than these' " (Mark 12:29-31).

Does your life purpose relate to the first commandment of loving God with all your heart, soul, mind, and strength? ☒ Yes ☐ No

Write a statement of your life purpose in relation to God.

To Love God more than I Love myself and my mother.

Jesus' second command gives you another clue to a life purpose—loving others as you love yourself. Loving your fellow human beings is second only to loving God. Your life purpose should relate to these two commands regardless of your job or profession. Everything you do should glorify God (see 1 Cor. 10:31; Col. 3:17; 1 Pet. 4:11).

Write a life purpose related to your fellow human beings.

Value every human being as I would myself.

This week's Scripture-memory verse, Ephesians 6:18, speaks to the issue of determining your life purpose. Turn to page 83 and read this verse aloud. What is one way to know the purpose God has for you?

Pray for all kinds of requests.

God desires to reveal His goal for you. Through prayer for all kinds of requests, He will hear you and answer you.

DEMOLISHING PERSONAL SPIRITUAL STRONGHOLDS

God wants your life to be free of personal strongholds, and He gives you the strength and the means to demolish them. You have examined the strongholds of bitterness, speech, lust, and religious ritual. Today look at the stronghold of greed in your life and prayerfully consider how the Lord might be directing you to demolish this stronghold.

Read the verses in the margin, which deal with the stronghold of greed. Greed, or covetousness, is an intense desire to possess something or someone that belongs to another person or to acquire more than you need. This desire springs from greedy self-centeredness and an arrogant disregard of God's law.

After you have read the Scripture verses, describe the area of greed in your life that needs to be demolished, what you need to do to demolish it, and the spiritual weapon(s) to be used in demolishing it. Later this week you will record your progress. Here is an example.

Stronghold to be demolished: spending too much time shopping—acquiring possessions or envisioning ways I can acquire them—and not enough time studying God's Word

What I need to do to demolish it: shop only for essentials; spend time developing my spiritual life

"Do not store up for yourselves treasures on earth, where moth and rust destroy, and where thieves break in and steal. But store up for yourselves treasures in heaven, where moth and rust do not destroy, and where thieves do not break in and steal. For where your treasure is, there your heart will be also. No one can serve two masters. Either he will hate the one and love the other, or he will be devoted to the one and despise the other. You cannot serve both God and Money. Therefore I tell you, do not worry about your life, what you will eat or drink; or about your body, what you will wear. Is not life more important than food, and the body more important than clothes? Look at the birds of the air; they do not sow or reap or store away in barns, and yet your heavenly Father feeds them. Are you not much more valuable than they? But seek first his kingdom and his righteousness, and all these things will be given to you as well" (Matt. 6:19-21,24-26,33).

Spiritual weapons to be used: Sword of the Spirit—to remind me of the need for heavenly, and not earthly, treasures; Breastplate of Righteousness—to claim God's protection to help me live rightly and to put my priorities in the right place; Shield of Faith—to help me believe that God will provide for my needs

Now you try it.

Stronghold to be demolished: Spending too much time thinking of how I can achieve earthly success

What I need to do to demolish it: spend more time developing my personal life and build my faith in God.

Spiritual weapon(s) to be used: Shield of Faith - to help me believe that God will provide for my needs. Sword of the Spirit - to remind me of the need for heavenly, and not earthly treasures.

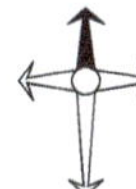

Begin preparing for the Prayer Workshop that will follow week 6 by developing a personal prayer journal. The following material will tell you how.

HOW TO DEVELOP YOUR PERSONAL PRAYER JOURNAL

Make your journal person. Because this article suggests that you copy items in this book and in books 1 and 2, you may wish to use an 8½-by-11-inch loose-leaf binder so that you can punch holes in the pages as you copy and file them under the categories listed. Even if you copy material from this book or from books 1 and 2, plan to bring your *MasterLife* books to the Prayer Workshop so that you can refer to your Daily Master Communication Guides.

Purposes of Your Personal Prayer Journal

1. To help you organize your personal life and your prayer life
2. To equip you to minister to your world through prayer
3. To remind you of what to pray about
4. To enable you to monitor your spiritual growth and walk

The Meaning of Your Personal Prayer Journal

1. *Personal* means that you should design and use a prayer journal that fits your particular needs and personality.
2. *Prayer* means that the focus should be on regularly meeting God in prayer, not on praying from habit.
3. *Journal* means that it is a guide and a record of your communication with God.

Design and use a prayer journal that fits your particular needs and personality.

You may wish to organize further the categories you have listed according to the frequency with which you will pray about different concerns.

Organizing Your Personal Prayer Journal

1. Prepare tabs in your notebook for three main divisions:
   a. Prayer Resources
   b. Prayer Lists
   c. Personal Guidance
2. *Prayer Resources.* Behind this tab insert copies of or notes about the locations of prayer resources you have studied in *MasterLife.* Later you may place additional resources behind this tab.
   a. The Disciple's Cross, book 1
   b. Prayer-Covenant List (to date), books 1, 2, and 3
   c. The Disciple's Personality, book 2
   d. "Principles of Conversational Prayer," book 2
   e. Weeks 2 and 4, book 3
   f. Relational-Witnessing Chart, book 3
   g. The Spiritual Armor, book 3
   h. "Guide to Thanksgiving," book 3
   i. "Guide to Praise," book 3
   j. "Guide to Confession and Forgiveness," book 3
   k. "Guide to Praying in Faith," book 3
   l. "Guide to Intercession," book 3
   m. "Guide to Extended Prayer," book 3
3. *Prayer Lists.* Behind this tab place tabs for two subdivisions: Categories and Calendar.
   a. *Categories.* Prepare separate pages for each of the following categories and place them behind the Categories tab. You may want to add other categories to meet your needs. Secure additional blank copies of the Prayer-Covenant List. Include your current Prayer-Covenant List, and your Relational-Witnessing Chart as a basis for determining the objects you will list under each category. Examples of categories:
      - family members
      - relatives
      - close friends
      - business associates
      - persons in authority
      - missionaries
      - church leaders
      - disciples
      - countries
   b. *Calendar.* You may wish to organize further the categories you have listed according to the frequency with which you will pray about different concerns. If so, move some of the preceding category pages or prepare separate pages as follows and place them behind the Calendar tab.
      - *Daily prayer list.* Include persons or items for which you pray every day, such as personal and family needs and missionaries.
      - *Weekly prayer list.* Arrange lists under the Categories tab so that you pray for a different category each day.
      - *Monthly prayer list.* Spend a half day or a day in prayer each month and review your prayer lists and answers.

- *Annual prayer list.* List your life purpose; your annual goals; and items for which you pray only annually, such as events on your church or denominational calendars and specific countries.

4. *Personal Guidance.* Behind this tab place the following lists, which you will learn to prepare in this week's study.
   a. *Life purpose.*
   b. *Life goals.*
   c. *Monthly goals.* Compile this list during your half or full day in prayer each month. Monthly goals should be specific and should contribute to life goals.
   d. *Weekly goals.* Develop this list during your weekly planning session. This is a sample list of weekly goals:
      - Read and mark my Bible 10 minutes a day.
      - Memorize a new verse each week.
      - Do physical exercise three times each week.
      - Have individual Bible study one hour each week.
      - Witness to one person each week.
      - Take notes on one sermon each week.
      - Have a half day of prayer each month.

      List your weekly goals on a chart like the one on page 143. You may record the time you spend in each activity or simply check the items when completed. Write the date for each day on a separate line. At the end of the day or at the beginning of the next day, fill in the items you have done, completing only the blanks that apply to that day. For example, the half day of prayer a month would be filled in only on the day you completed that activity.

Using Your Personal Prayer Journal

1. Begin where you are and develop your journal as you go.
2. Use your personal prayer journal each day.
   a. Pray for persons on your daily prayer list.
   b. Pray for the particular prayer-list category you have designated for that day.
   c. Mark your personal-guidance list each day.
3. Plan to spend a half day in prayer once a month.
4. Plan an annual evaluation time.
5. Keep developing your personal prayer journal to fit you.

Read Psalm 119:121-128 during your quiet time today. Let God speak to you through this passage. Then complete the Daily Master Communication Guide in the margin.

Daily Master Communication Guide

Psalm 119:121-128

What God said to me:

Ask me for discernment so you can understand my laws (ways). Allow me to teach you my ways so you will better understand what I desire of you.

What I said to God:

I pray O God that you will give me discernment so that I will understand your ways O God. Teach me your laws and give me understanding so that I will not be lead astray, but will stay on your path O God. Thank you.

DAY 2

In Line with God's Will

On our third furlough from missionary service in Indonesia God revealed to me through prayer and Scripture that He wanted me to join the staff of my denomination's discipleship ministry. In that position I would develop *MasterLife* and LIFE courses, which would equip God's people to serve Him and go on mission with Him to all peoples of the world. As I was preparing to talk with the staff of my denomination's publishing house in detail, God impressed me with Exodus 18:14-27, in which Moses received helpful counsel from his father-in-law, Jethro. When I read his words to Moses in verses 19-21, I felt that God was speaking to me, and I began to consider how.

The first thing He showed me was in verse 19: "Listen now to me and I will give you some advice, and may God be with you. You must be the people's representative before God and bring their disputes to him." I sensed God telling me that I should be an intercessor for His people and that I should bring their causes, or issues, before Him.

The second teaching was easy to understand, because it related to what I anticipated doing in *MasterLife*. Verse 20 says, "Teach them the decrees and laws, and show them the way to live and the duties they are to perform." "Teach them" and "show them" are discipleship. "The way to live and the duties they are to perform" are the content of discipleship and ministry.

The third point confused me. Moses was told to choose people to lead who would be rulers of thousands, hundreds, fifties, and tens (see v. 21). Although I would be supervising a few persons in this new task, that in no way compared to what this Scripture seemed to indicate. Over the next 15 years I wondered if this referred to the numerous *MasterLife* leaders and trainers. Yet I often wondered if God had more for me to do that related to this third part of the Bible promise.

The result of this soul-searching about my life was that I had to wait for 15 years until God prepared me and led me to my present position at our denomination's International Mission Board. My main responsibility is to direct the work of more than 4,000 missionaries and 15,000 volunteers each year around the world by working with 14 regional leaders. Each regional leader works with approximately 300 missionaries in up to 25 missions in each region. They are organized on the local-station or unit level, which is similar to the small unit in Moses' time.

We often do not understand what God has in mind when He begins to share with us what He wants to do with our lives. If we remain faithful to Him, He shows us how He wants to fulfill His purpose in us. Many times He opens our vision to what He is planning through a Scripture He places on our hearts.

If we remain faithful to Him, He shows us how He wants to fulfill His purpose in us.

SETTING LIFE GOALS

Many people talk about discovering God's will for their lives. God says that His will is bringing the world to Himself. That includes salvation and sanctification for all who accept Him.

Read 2 Peter 3:9, 1 Timothy 2:3-4, and 1 Thessalonians 4:3 in the margin. Underline the statement in each verse that reveals God's will to us.

"The Lord is not slow in keeping his promise, as some understand slowness. He is patient with you, not wanting anyone to perish, but everyone to come to repentance" (2 Pet. 3:9).

"This is good, and pleases God our Savior, who wants all men to be saved and to come to a knowledge of the truth" (1 Tim. 2:3-4).

"It is God's will that you should be sanctified" (1 Thess. 4:3).

You do not have to discover the overarching aspects of God's will. He has revealed them. Your life purpose should relate to the salvation of the world and the sanctification of God's people. After you settle your life purpose, then you may concentrate on life goals by asking how you can best carry out God's will in your decisions about marriage, occupation, and other areas of your life.

A life purpose is an overarching goal for you to accomplish in your lifetime. It provides direction for everyday activities and determines your priorities. A life goal is a specific objective for an important area of your life. Achieving all of your life goals should equal achieving your life purpose.

Read the following decisions and write *purpose* beside those that relate to life purpose and *goal* beside steps to achieve life goals.

goal ____ **1. Choosing a good vocation**
goal ____ **2. Marrying a Christian**
Purpose ____ **3. Living for God's glory**
Purpose ____ **4. Serving persons in need**
goal ____ **5. Using my home as a base for ministry**
~~Purpose~~ goal ____ **6. Accepting myself as God accepts me**

A purpose is something that is clearly in line with God's revealed will; goals represent ways to carry out God's will. Statements 3 and 4 relate to life purpose and statements 1, 2, 5, and 6 to life goals.

Mark 12:29-31, with which you became familiar in day 1, illustrates a believer's life purpose. If you love God, you want to be like Him. You want to achieve His purposes. If you love those around you, you want them to have all God intended for them, including eternal life.

If you love God, you want to be like Him. You want to achieve His purposes.

Can you recall from day 1 the two broad purposes for a believer's life that are listed in Mark 12:29-31? Look back at the verses on page 85 if you need to refresh your memory.

① Love the Lord your God with all your heart and with all your soul and with all your mind and with all your strength.

② Love your neighbor as yourself.

You need life goals and convictions about what God wants you to do as you move in faith with Him to achieve His purposes.

These purposes are overarching objectives on which you can bank your life. To achieve God's purposes, it is necessary to have intermediate life goals that lead to the ultimate objective. You need life goals and convictions about what God wants you to do as you move in faith with Him to achieve His purposes.

Jesus' life purposes were to glorify the Father and to accomplish God's plan for the redemption of humankind. To achieve those purposes, He set life goals, described in John 17, that included—

- revealing the Father;
- reconciling the world to Himself;
- discipling those the Father gave Him to carry out His work.

Explain your understanding of the relationship between life purpose and life goals.

Personal life goals lead to the accomplishment of your life purpose.

Ephesians 6:18, this week's Scripture-memory verse, says to pray about "all kinds of prayers and requests." Do you believe that verse of Scripture applies to requests for revealing life goals to you? ☑ Yes ❑ No Say the verse aloud from one to three times to remind yourself of this promise.

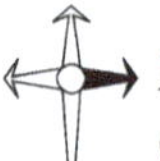

Mark 12:29-31 mentions loving your neighbor. Show God's love to someone every day this week.

One of Jesus' life goals was to accomplish His Father's purpose for the redemption of humanity. Is this your purpose? If so, the next piece of the Spiritual Armor will help you accomplish this purpose.

PUTTING ON THE SPIRITUAL ARMOR

This week's study focuses on the Gospel Shoes part of the Spiritual Armor presentation—feet fitted with the readiness that comes from the gospel of peace. Turn to pages 129–31 and review the Spiritual Armor presentation, with special emphasis on the soldier's fitted feet. By the end of this study you will be able to explain the entire presentation in your own words.

Picture the soldier's studded sandals on your feet. The preparation of the gospel of peace means that you are ready for battle. It reminds you to do three things:

Get ready before the battle begins.

1. Be prepared. Get ready before the battle begins. Pray that God will prepare you for any possibility.
2. Share the gospel. The readiness that comes from the gospel of peace means to be ready to proclaim the gospel. Ask God to prepare you to witness for Him.

3. Intercede for the lost. You are prepared to attack the enemy through prayer or witness. Paul was effective in witness because he prayed for the lost (see Rom. 10:1). Pray for lost friends on your prayer lists. Visualize the countries of the world, with their millions of lost people, and pray for their salvation.

Focus on the first of the three reminders. Stop and ask God to prepare you for whatever battles come your way today.

GOD'S WORD IN YOUR HEART AND HAND

In the two previous weeks you have learned to imagine yourself grasping God's Word in your hand as you hold the Sword of the Spirit, God's Word. The Bible uses several illustrations for the Word that suggest why a firm grasp of the Word is necessary for effective application.

Read the section "Level 3: Illustration" (p. 134) in the God's Word in Your Heart and Hand presentation. Then record the symbols that the presentation mentions. As you write each, explain how it relates to the grasp you have on the Word.

1. Food - The word is able to nourish me and satisfy my spiritual hunger. I am able to use it to feed others.
2. Light - the word is a light that guides me in the dark so I don't stumble and fall. I can light the lamps for others with my light.
3. Fire -
4. Sword - The word of God cuts through every barrier to expose everything that is not of God. It judges the thoughts and attitudes of the heart.

Select one level of the God's Word in Your Heart and Hand presentation and share it with your family or a Christian friend.

Read Psalm 119:129-136 during your quiet time today. Then complete the Daily Master Communication Guide in the margin.

Daily Master Communication Guide

Psalm 119:129-136

What God said to me:

Dig deep into my word and you will find the wisdom that you desire. You will find understanding when you explore the words that I have spoken. Allow my word to be your light that guides your footsteps in these dark times.

What I said to God:

Please Help me Lord to dive into your word to seek the wisdom that I desire of you Lord. Help me to take my time in exploring your word so that I can have understanding. Help me to let your word be my light for my feet, so I won't stumble and fall, or cause anyone else to fall.

DAY 3

Achieving God's Purposes

An Old Testament account illustrates the importance of having a life purpose and life goals. Read Joshua 14:6-14 in the margin. Joshua and Caleb were the 2 spies who gave a positive report in Numbers 13, while the other 10 spies did not believe that God would defeat the people in the promised land.

Although Caleb had to wander through the wilderness for 45 years after Israel refused to conquer Canaan, he had a purpose that kept him going. He had a mountain God wanted him to claim. As they entered the promised land, Caleb said: "This is my job. I want the mountain God promised me."

Match the following questions and answers.

___ 1. What was Caleb's life purpose?	**a. The large, fortified enemy cities were unconquerable without God.**
___ 2. What was Caleb's specific life goal?	**b. A promise from God about his life goal**
___ 3. How do you know that his goal was ordained by God?	**c. The achieving of his life goal fulfilled his life purpose.**
___ 4. What was the basis of Caleb's faith?	**d. To follow the Lord fully**
___ 5. How did his goal fit with his life purpose?	**e. To take the land as his inheritance**

Caleb was committed to following the Lord fully. That was his life purpose. His life goal was to take the land as his inheritance, which God had ordained and promised him through Moses. The goal was impossible without the Lord's help because the enemy cities were large, fortified, and unconquerable without God. His acquisition of Hebron as an inheritance glorified God and signified that Caleb had followed the Lord wholeheartedly. The correct answers are 1. d, 2. e, 3. a, 4. b, 5. c.

CHARACTERISTICS OF LIFE GOALS

Caleb's goals have three important characteristics that should also characterize your goals:

1. Life goals are God-revealed rather than conceived by you.
2. Life goals are too big to achieve without God's power.
3. Life goals arrange your life so that you can achieve your life purpose.

"Now the men of Judah approached Joshua at Gilgal, and Caleb son of Jephunneh the Kenizzite said to him, 'You know what the Lord said to Moses the man of God at Kadesh Barnea about you and me. I was forty years old when Moses the servant of the Lord sent me from Kadesh Barnea to explore the land. And I brought him back a report according to my convictions, but my brothers who went up with me made the hearts of the people melt with fear. I, however, followed the Lord my God wholeheartedly. So on that day Moses swore to me, "The land on which your feet have walked will be your inheritance and that of your children forever, because you have followed the Lord my God wholeheartedly." Now then, just as the Lord promised, he has kept me alive for forty-five years since the time he said this to Moses, while Israel moved about in the desert. So here I am today, eighty-five years old! I am still as strong today as the day Moses sent me out; I'm just as vigorous to go out to battle now as I was then. Now give me this hill country that the Lord promised me that day. You yourself heard then that the Anakites were there and their cities were large and fortified, but the Lord helping me, I will drive them out just as he said.' Then Joshua blessed Caleb son of Jephunneh and gave him Hebron as his inheritance. So Hebron has belonged to Caleb son of Jephunneh the

Kenizzite ever since, because he followed the Lord, the God of Israel, wholeheartedly" (Josh. 14:6-14).

Consider the first characteristic: Life goals are God-revealed rather than conceived by you. Read Matthew 16:21-23 in the margin. Write *G* beside the God-revealed goal and *H* beside the goal conceived by human beings.

G **Jesus would suffer, die, and rise again.**

H **Jesus would remain with them as an earthly king.**

"From that time on Jesus began to explain to his disciples that he must go to Jerusalem and suffer many things at the hands of the elders, chief priests and teachers of the law, and that he must be killed and on the third day be raised to life. Peter took him aside and began to rebuke him. 'Never, Lord!' he said. 'This shall never happen to you.' Jesus turned and said to Peter, 'Get behind me, Satan! You are a stumbling block to me; you do not have in mind the things of God, but the things of men'" (Matt. 16:21-23).

Obviously, Jesus' followers conceived their own ideas about what direction His life should take. They wanted to set a goal for Him that He would remain with them and reign on earth. But Jesus operated by a God-revealed goal—that he must be killed and rise from the dead. You have also seen that Caleb's life goal came from God.

Now look at the second characteristic: Life goals are too big to achieve without God's power. Only God's power working in you can propel you to achieve your goals. At 85 years of age Caleb could not conquer the giants in his country by human strength. In Colossians 1:28 Paul stated that his goal was to present everyone perfect in Christ. In the next verse he explained how he would accomplish this: "To this end I labor, struggling with all his energy, which so powerfully works in me" (Col. 1:29).

Why do you think God wants to be the power source for achieving His purposes?

Because we are limited in our human abilities and will be able to accomplish His purpose without Him.

God wants you to depend on Him. He receives the glory of working through you. Because of your sinfulness and humanity, you are limited in what you can do. You cannot do God's work without His help. He wants His energy to work powerfully in you. John 15:5 says that apart from Him, you can do nothing.

Recall the third characteristic: Life goals arrange your life so that you can achieve your life purpose. What do you think kept Caleb going those 45 years as he wandered with the disobedient Israelites? He could have said: "God, why do I have to stay in the wilderness with these turkeys? I believe that You could have led us into the promised land long ago." However, because he stayed focused on his life goals and held on to God's promise to him, he was ready to take the promised land in God's time.

Remembering your life goals helps you order your priorities. Many times your choices are not between good and evil but between good and best. Satan often wants you to settle for merely good things if that keeps you from waiting for God's best gifts.

Remembering your life goals helps you order your priorities.

See if you can list the three characteristics of life goals.

1. God revealed rather than conceived by you

DAILY MASTER COMMUNICATION GUIDE

PSALM 119:137-144

What God said to me:

Allow my word to be your source of energy when you feel burnt out and feel like you can't go anymore. Don't the response you receive from others to discourage you. Allow my word to motivate you to keep pushing forward.

What I said to God:

Thank you Lord that I have your word as my power source, so that I will always find strength when I feel burnt out and done. Allow me to not be discouraged by the response that I receive from people ~~but~~ always holding on to your word to motivate me and keep me going.

2. Too big to achieve without God's power.

3. Arrange your life so that you can achieve your life purpose.

When you make important choices in life, such as your vocation or marriage partner, ask yourself, *Will this choice help me achieve God's purpose for my life?* If so, it is worthy of your efforts to attain it. If you set life goals without first determining your life purpose, you often substitute your goals for God's purposes.

When you set worthy goals, it is as though you put on a new set of glasses to view your future. In the long run, a worthy goal will bring you peace, will help you look at things in a long-term way, will keep you focused, and will help you measure all things in light of God's purposes.

Caleb followed God fully in taking possession of Hebron. Jesus followed God fully in revealing the Father, in reconciling the world to Himself, and in discipling those who would carry out His work.

What evidence do you have that the goals you presently work toward will accomplish your life purpose?

____

PUTTING ON THE SPIRITUAL ARMOR

In day 2 you learned the importance of putting on the Gospel Shoes as you continued learning the Spiritual Armor presentation. You learned three steps for having your feet fitted with the readiness that comes from the gospel of peace. Review the reminders on pages 92–93.

Focus on the second reminder. Stop and ask God to make you ready to witness for Him.

One way you can be prepared for a witnessing situation is to have God's Word at instant recall. You have been memorizing Scriptures throughout your study of *MasterLife*. If you studied book 1, you learned suggestions for memorizing Scripture. You may want to refer to that guide as you continue your Scripture-memory work.

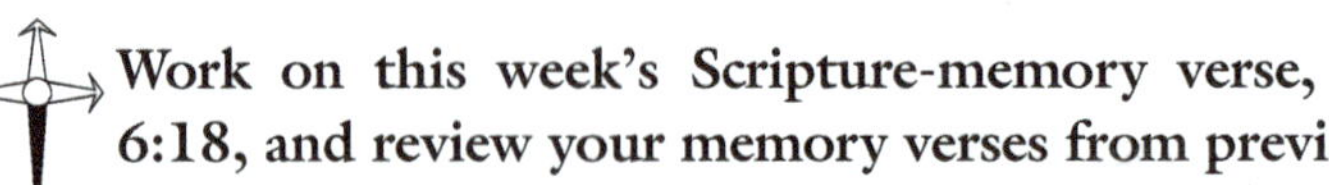

Work on this week's Scripture-memory verse, Ephesians 6:18, and review your memory verses from previous weeks.

Read Psalm 119:137-144 during your quiet time today. Let God speak to you through this passage. Then complete the Daily Master Communication Guide in the margin.

Pray in the Spirit on all occassions with all kinds of prayers and requests. With this in mind, be alert, always keep on praying for all the saints. Eph 6:18

DAY 4

Learning to Set Priorities

After you have determined your life purpose and have totally committed yourself to Christ in carrying out those purposes, you can move with clarity to set priorities. Loving God and loving your neighbor are the overarching objectives toward which you always move in your life purpose. Every time you make a decision, involve yourself in a relationship, or invest time or money, check it against your life purpose. If you question whether a particular action truly moves you toward accomplishing your life purpose, you may need to reconsider the action.

Every time you make a decision, involve yourself in a relationship, or invest time or money, check it against your life purpose.

TOWARD MATURITY

The Phillips version of the Scriptures translates Romans 12:2 as follows: "Don't let the world around you squeeze you into its own mold, but let God remold your minds from within, so that you may prove in practice that the plan of God for you is good, meets all His demands, and moves toward the goal of true maturity." God's plan is that you move toward maturity.

In the Scripture above, underline the three things God is doing to remold your mind as His purpose for your life.

The verse says that as God remolds you, you can prove in practice that God's plan for you is good, meets all of His demands, and moves toward the goal of true maturity.

What do the verses in the margin say that a growing disciple does? Match each reference with the corresponding statement.

__ 1. Philippians 2:5	**a. Knows his or her responsibility and acts on it**
__ 2. Colossians 3:1-2	**b. Is equipped with the mind of Christ**
__ 3 Ephesians 5:15	**c. Has high priorities**

"Your attitude should be the same as that of Christ Jesus" (Phil. 2:5).

"Since, then, you have been raised with Christ, set your hearts on things above, where Christ is seated at the right hand of God. Set your minds on things above, not on earthly things" (Col. 3:1-2).

"Live life, then, with a due sense of responsibility, not as men who do not know the meaning of life but as those who do" (Eph. 5:15, Phillips).

Knowing where you are going in life is exciting when you have the mind of Christ and engage it, know what your responsibility is and do it, and have high priorities. The answers are 1. b, 2. c, 3. a.

Your next concern is to develop a plan for moving toward accomplishing your life purpose.

HOW TO SET PRIORITIES

The following diagram shows what your priorities should be. Ask yourself, *What is God most concerned about in my life? What is His priority for me?* The diagram depicts basic life goals—the major items that form the framework for building a life under God's plan. A definite order exists for developing these goals.

Most people make the mistake of starting at the top with mate and career before they set the previous four goals in the sequence shown in the diagram. Note how the priorities progress. First is the foundation.

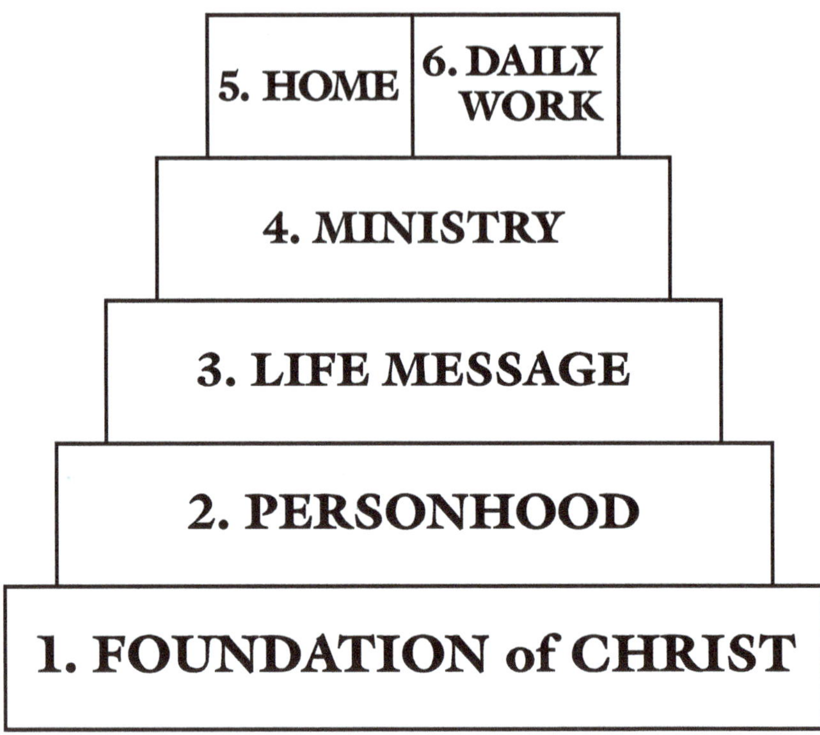

"Just as you received Christ Jesus as Lord, continue to live in him, rooted and built up in him, strengthened in the faith as you were taught, and overflowing with thankfulness" (Col. 2:6-7).

Read Colossians 2:6-7 in the margin. In whom are you to live and build your life after you receive Christ as your Savior and Lord?

In Christ
___

"No one can lay any foundation other than the one already laid, which is Jesus Christ. If any man builds on this foundation using gold, silver, costly stones, wood, hay or straw, his work will be shown for what it is, because the Day will bring it to light. It will be revealed with fire, and the fire will test the quality of each man's work" (1 Cor. 3:11-13).

THE FOUNDATION OF CHRIST

Build and root your life in Jesus Christ. He is the foundation of your life. First Corinthians 3:11-13, in the margin, presents an analogy Paul used to illustrate the concept of building a life on Jesus Christ. You first begin with the foundation and then select the building materials. You, as the builder, are responsible for the building itself and the permanence of the materials selected. When it is completed, the Building Inspector will examine it.

Be certain that you build every aspect of your life on Jesus Christ. The life goal that relates to this building block answers the question, *Are Christ and His kingdom my first priority?*

In the blank pyramid on the following page write *foundation of Christ* and *Matthew 6:33* on the lower building block.

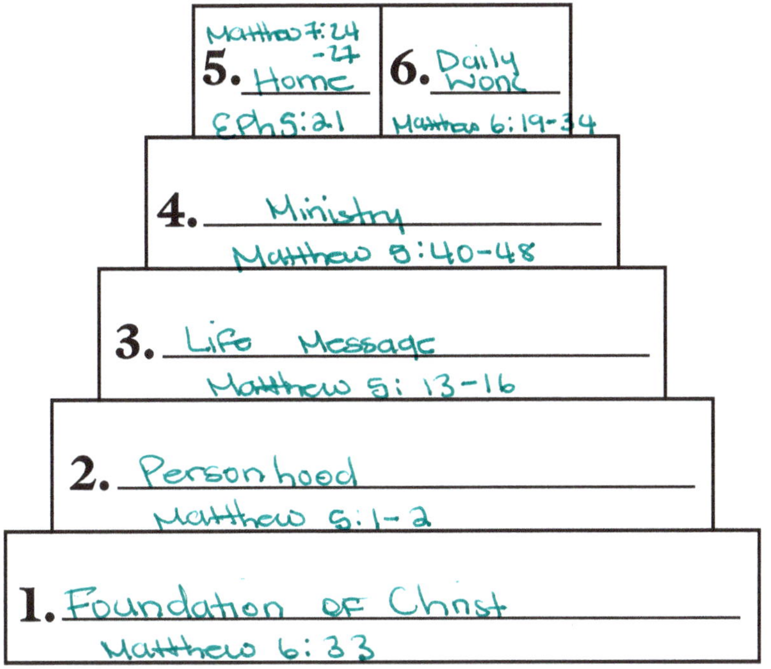

PERSONHOOD

The first building block to be placed on the foundation of Christ is you. God is primarily concerned about you.

Write *personhood* and *Matthew 5:1-12* on the second block of the pyramid.

God wants to guide you to become all He intended. He is more concerned about the kind of person you become than about what career you choose. He is more concerned about inner qualities than about how you look. This second building block deals with life goals that answer the question, *What kind of person am I becoming?*

God begins with the task of producing in you the character of Jesus Christ. Until this begins to happen, Christ cannot use you effectively.

If you are not clear about the kind of person God wants you to be, read the following passages of Scripture.

- **Psalm 139:13-16**
- **Matthew 6:33**
- **Luke 2:52**
- **Acts 24:16**
- **Romans 12:1-2**
- **1 Corinthians 12:7**
- **2 Corinthians 5:17**
- **Galatians 5:22-23**
- **Ephesians 5:18**
- **Colossians 3:1-17**
- **1 Thessalonians 4:1-8**
- **1 Peter 3:3-4**
- **1 John 5:11-13**

Say aloud this week's Scripture-memory verse, Ephesians 6:18. Do you believe helping you set life goals is included in "all kinds of prayers and requests"? ☒ Yes ☐ No If so, stop and ask God to help you in this process of determining goals.

Daily Master Communication Guide

Psalm 119:145-152

What God said to me:

Put your hope in my word because it will never fail and it lasts forever. Allow my words to be your comfort, your refuge, and your strength in times of need.

What I said to God:

Dear God, please help me to put all my hope in your word because your word never failed and will never fail. Please let your word be my comfort, my refuge, and my strength so that I will not fail.

PUTTING ON THE SPIRITUAL ARMOR

This week you have learned the importance of putting on the Gospel Shoes as you have continued learning the Spiritual Armor presentation. Review on pages 92–93 the three steps you learned for having your feet fitted with the readiness that comes from the gospel of peace.

Focus on the third reminder. Stop and pray that lost friends will have Christ as the foundation for their lives. Then visualize the countries of the world, with their millions of lost people, and pray for their salvation.

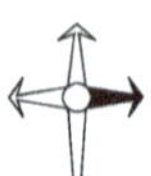

Share with your family, a Christian friend, or a group the Gospel Shoes part of the Spiritual Armor.

As you pray, use "Guide to Intercession," which follows.

"I urge, then, first of all, that requests, prayers, intercession and thanksgiving be made for everyone" (1 Tim. 2:1).

"... for kings and all those in authority, that we may live peaceful and quiet lives in all godliness and holiness. This is good, and pleases God our Savior, who wants all men to be saved and to come to a knowledge of the truth" (1 Tim. 2:2-4).

"There is one God and one mediator between God and men, the man Christ Jesus, who gave himself as a ransom for all men—the testimony given in its proper time. And for this purpose I was appointed a herald and an apostle—I am telling the truth, I am not lying—and a teacher of the true faith to the Gentiles" (1 Tim. 2:5-7).

"I want men everywhere to lift up holy hands in prayer, without anger or disputing" (1 Tim. 2:8).

GUIDE TO INTERCESSION

Intercession is the ministry of a disciple and the community of faith to bring to God the needs of the church and the world. It can result in changed lives, changed churches, and a changed world.

Begin a ministry of intercession by following these suggestions.

1. Make intercession your first priority (see 1 Tim. 2:1 in the margin). Spend much of your prayer time in intercession.
2. Use all types of prayers in your intercession, combining praise, thanksgiving, requests, and intercession.
3. Intercede for all people (see 1 Tim. 2:2-4 in the margin).
4. Intercede with an all-embracing purpose. Intercession is not limited to specific life needs and crises. Intercession should seek salvation, peace, godliness, quietness, and holiness for all people (see 1 Tim. 2:5-7 in the margin).
5. Pray in unity with other disciples (see 1 Tim. 2:8 in the margin).
6. Pray on the basis of God's character.
7. Stand before God in place of the person in need, ready to sacrifice yourself to have the need met, as Moses, Paul, and Jesus did.
8. Persevere until you prevail.
9. Remember that the Lord Himself is your partner in intercession (see John 17; Rom. 8:26-27).
10. Remain confident, for the promise of intercession is sure (see Matt. 7:7; Jas. 5:16).

Read Psalm 119:145-152 during your quiet time today. Let God speak to you through this passage. Then complete the Daily Master Communication Guide in the margin on page 99.

DAY 5

Building a Life for God

Yesterday you learned the foundation block for determining your life goals, and you studied the first block for building a life according to God's plan. Today you will study the remaining four blocks.

LIFE MESSAGE

The next building block you place on the foundation of Christ is your life message.

Write *life message* and *Matthew 5:13-16* in the third block in the pyramid on page 99.

The life goals you write at this level answer the questions: *What do others see in my life? What does my life say to others?* Your life message grows from your personhood. If you are truly becoming a Christlike person, those who know you and observe your life see it. Your life message is the signpost that reveals to others who you really are. They recognize your realness and sincerity. You are your life message. Your life message is the total of your experiences from which you can speak with authority because you have done what you said. It characterizes how others perceive you.

In my first pastorate I hoped that people would remember the messages I preached. Then I noticed what the members said about previous pastors. They never mentioned their messages but made comments like "Brother Jones really loved people," "Brother Smith was a great prayer," and "Brother Tom was a walking Bible." Each was a life message!

Read Matthew 5:16 in the margin. Who gets the credit when you live as a shining light (a Christlike example) before others?

God -> Your Father in heaven
___

Even though people may see good qualities in you, the source of all good in you is your Father in heaven. Your life message should reflect Him and honor Him. You develop this message when you make Christ the center of your life, when you internalize God's Word, and when you develop your spiritual gifts.

MINISTRY

Ministry flows from your personhood and your life message. It is a natural overflow, not a forced effort. As you drink the water Jesus gives, an overflow will naturally occur. Read Matthew 5:40-48 in the margin.

"Let your light shine before men, that they may see your good deeds and praise your Father in heaven" (Matt. 5:16).

"If someone wants to sue you and take your tunic, let him have your cloak as well. If someone forces you to go one mile, go with him two miles. Give to the one who asks you, and do not turn away from the one who wants to borrow from you. You have heard that it was said, 'Love your neighbor and hate your enemy.' But I tell you: Love your enemies and pray for those who persecute you, that you may be sons of your Father in heaven. He causes his sun to rise on the evil and the good, and sends rain on the righteous and the unrighteous. If you love those who love you, what reward will you get? Are not even the tax collectors doing that? And if you greet only your brothers, what are you doing more than others? Do not even pagans do that? Be perfect, therefore, as your heavenly Father is perfect" (Matt. 5:40-48).

Write *ministry* and *Matthew 5:40-48* on the fourth block in the pyramid on page 99.

Ministry answers the question, *How can I share my life with others?* The verses in the margin give ideas about life goals involving ministry.

"You are the salt of the earth. But if the salt loses it saltiness, how can it be made salty again? It is no longer good for anything, except to be thrown out and trampled by men" (Matt. 5:13).

"Each one should use whatever gift he has received to serve others, faithfully administering God's grace in its various forms" (1 Pet. 4:10).

"You will receive power when the Holy Spirit comes on you; and you will be my witnesses in Jerusalem, and in all Judea and Samaria, and to the ends of the earth" (Acts 1:8).

"Let us consider how we may spur one another on toward love and good deeds. Let us not give up meeting together, as some are in the habit of doing, but let us encourage one another—and all the more as you see the Day approaching" (Heb. 10:24-25).

"We proclaim him, admonishing and teaching everyone with all wisdom, so that we may present everyone perfect in Christ" (Col. 1:28-29).

"Be joyful in hope, patient in affliction, faithful in prayer. Share with God's people who are in need. Practice hospitality" (Rom. 12:12-13).

Read the verses in the margin and match their references with the ideas they convey.

E 1. Matthew 5:13	**a. Using the gifts God gave you**
A 2. 1 Peter 4:10	**b. Sharing Christ**
B 3. Acts 1:8	**c. Making disciples**
D 4. Hebrews 10:24-25	**d. Serving through the church**
C 5. Colossians 1:28-29	**e. Penetrating your part of the secular world**
F 6. Romans 12:12-13	**f. Meeting human needs**

God has called you to a life of ministry. No disciple is exempt from this call. Concentrate on walking with Christ and on becoming like Him. Learn to see people through His eyes, and He will give you a ministry. The correct answers are 1. e, 2. a, 3. b, 4. d, 5. c, 6. f.

HOME

Your home is a vital part of your ministry.

Read the verses in the margin on page 103. On what should both a marital union and a home be based?

Christ

Write *home*, *Ephesians 5:21*, and *Matthew 7:24-27* on the top left block in the pyramid on page 99.

Christ is the foundation of a wise person's home and the center of our home relationships. Your home is the most natural place to demonstrate what Christ is doing in your life and will do in others' lives. The home may speak to the world more quickly than the church does. The question is, *How can I make my home a platform for my ministry?*

Both married and single persons should consider how their special circumstances can best contribute to their life goals. A growing disciple who is planning marriage should never consider marrying a person who does not have a similar concept of building a life and a relationship on Christ. For those who seek a life partner, the home building block answers the question, *Who is the best person I can marry in order to have the most effective ministry together?*

For Christians, marriage is a partnership, a spiritual union of two persons whose chief desire in life is to glorify God and to become like Jesus Christ. First Peter 3:7 calls husband and wife the "joint heirs of the grace of life" (RSV). Priscilla and Aquila (see Rom. 16:3-5) understood their marriage in this light and used their home as a gathering place for the church. If you are married, determine to build your marriage into a relationship that becomes a penetrating witness in the world and that shows Christ's power in true love and purpose. For a married couple, the question is, *How does God intend to use our relationship in ministry together?*

You do not have to be married to be Christ's follower or to minister. If you are single, the question is, *How can I use my singleness to increase my ministry?* Your home is still a focal point for ministry.

"Submit to one another out of reverence for Christ" (Eph. 5:21).

"Everyone who hears these words of mine and puts them into practice is like a wise man who built his house on the rock" (Matt. 7:24).

DAILY WORK

You can gain a new vision for the way God can use you as an influence in your career or job by studying Matthew 6:19-34.

Write *daily work* and *Matthew 6:19-34* on the top right block in the pyramid on page 99.

The daily-work building block answers the question, *How can I allow Christ to use my career to minister?* Or if you are deciding on a career or employment, it answers the question, *What career would best enable me to have an effective ministry in the world?* Look at your daily work as one of the focal points of your ministry.

If believers followed this concept, it would literally revolutionize the secular work world. Whatever your job, work at it with all your heart, as serving the Lord and not the paycheck. Instead of goofing off or complaining, exhibit the spirit of Christ in attitudes, relationships, work habits, and decision making. The salt can penetrate the day-by-day work world, enabling you to touch people's lives significantly by the way you work. When they see your message, they will be open to ministry.

Whatever your job, work at it with all your heart, as serving the Lord.

Read the following prayer. Then pray it either by reading it aloud or by saying a similar prayer in your own words.

Lord, as I go to work, give me a vision of what You want me to be and do to influence my coworkers for Jesus Christ. Help me live in such a way that my message will be clear yet gentle and not overbearing. Help me demonstrate genuine love and be aware of opportunities You give for ministry and verbal witness. Help me make my job a penetrating point of my ministry for You in the world.

As you consider your present or prospective career, be sure that you are willing to change your career direction or to consider a call to a church-related ministry if God leads.

In *MasterLife 4: The Disciple's Mission* you will spend more time considering what God wants to accomplish in the world through you.

KEY QUESTIONS
- **What kind of person am I becoming?**
- **What do others see in my life? What does my life say to others?**
- **How can I share my life with others?**
- **How can I make my home a platform for my ministry? Who is the best person I can marry in order to have the most effective ministry together? How does God intend to use our relationship in ministry together? or How can I use my singleness to increase my ministry?**
- **How can I allow Christ to use my career to minister? or What career would best enable me to have an effective ministry in the world?**

Apply what you have learned this week by writing one major life goal related to each of the following building blocks. Refer to the questions in the margin as you write your goals. Then number your goals in the order of increasing priority.

Personhood: Teach personal bible study to the unsaved.

Message: Be mindful of my presentation to others.

Ministry: Do good to everyone, even those who hate me.

Home: Ensure that my home has a foundation built on god.

Daily work: Prioritize to seek and do the things of god.

DEMOLISHING PERSONAL SPIRITUAL STRONGHOLDS

In day 1 you identified a stronghold you wanted to demolish in the area of greed. Today give a progress report on how you have used the spiritual weapon(s) you listed to demolish this stronghold.

How I have used a spiritual weapon(s) to demolish the stronghold of greed:

Shield of faith to help me believe that god will provide for all my needs. Sword of the spirit to remind me of the need for heavenly treasures, not earthly ones.

You have probably become more aware of your need to witness.

Some people cannot build their life goals on a foundation of Christ because they have never heard the gospel message. As you have listed the names of lost persons on your Relational-Witnessing Chart, you have probably become more aware of your need to witness to those with whom you come in contact.

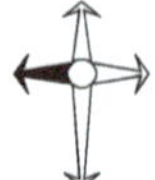

After reading "Expanding Your Witness Circle" on the following pages, continue adding names to the Relational-Witnessing Chart (p. 135) and to the Prayer-Covenant List (p. 143).

EXPANDING YOUR WITNESS CIRCLE

Begin expanding your witness circle by witnessing to the persons with whom you have close relationships, but do not stop there. Enlarge your circles of influence to include Person X. Person X is any person or any group of persons outside your circles of friends and associates with whom you could form a relationship. Minister to this person's needs and cultivate the friendship.

Jesus demonstrated the principles of lifestyle witnessing when He met the Samaritan woman (see John 4).[1] Follow His pattern as you design your personal strategy for lifestyle witnessing.

Relate to Lost Persons and Cultivate Witnessing Relationships

1. Geographically. Examine your traffic patterns. Are you going out of your way to cultivate witnessing relationships?
2. Socially. Examine your social relationships. The longer people have been church members, the fewer friends they have outside the church. Plan your calendar to ensure that you spend sufficient time cultivating relationships. Use your home to increase your witnessing opportunities by—

- inviting persons to dinner;
- having small-group fellowships in which a brief testimony is shared and individual conversations follow;
- holding Bible-study fellowships;
- offering special classes such as sewing, cooking, piano, nutrition, money management, arts, crafts, or drama;
- forming special clubs such as reading clubs;
- inviting newcomers in the community;
- being available for counseling;
- tutoring.

Relate to Felt Needs

As you talk with others, you often hear them express basic needs like love, self-esteem, meaning, a sense of security, and assurance of an afterlife. These can be avenues for ministry as well as for the verbal communication of the gospel.

Help Them Understand Their Real Need

Help people see their need for a personal relationship with Christ. Otherwise, they may never associate their loneliness or heartache with their need for Christ. As you deepen your relationships, share the way Christ has satisfied the deepest longings of your soul.

Maintain a Spirit of Acceptance

Although you do not approve of the lifestyle, maintain a spirit of love and compassion. Your concept of sanctification is faulty if you think that Christians should be isolated from the world (see John 17:15). Jesus was the friend of sinners.

Enlarge your circles of influence to include Person X.

Help people see their need for a personal relationship with Christ.

Daily Master Communication Guide

Psalm 119:153-160

What God said to me:

My promise is to free you from your sins and to protect you from all harm. You know my words are true, allow them to marinate in your heart so you will not feel alone or defeated, but strengthened and empowered.

What I said to God:

thank you God for your promise to free me from all my sins and to protect me from all harm. Please help me to hide your word in my heart so I will never for it and always have it on hand when in need.

Guide Them to Understand the Implications of the Gospel
Do not communicate that salvation is a matter of having the right religion. As you witness, always focus on the need of a personal relationship with Christ. Avoid discussing the merits of one religion over another.

Maintain a sense of urgency about leading persons to Christ. However, if they do not understand the implications of the gospel when it is first presented to them, continue to share patiently as the Holy Spirit works in their hearts. One woman said of another, "She built a bridge from her heart to mine, and Jesus Christ walked across." That is what witnessing is all about.

Are you building relationships? Check the statements that apply.

- ☒ **I refrain from being judgmental about another person's lifestyle.**
- ☐ **I enlist prayer partners to pray for my witnessing opportunities.**
- ☒ **I look for opportunities to share what Christ has done for me.**
- ☒ **I try to be patient while Christ works in others' hearts if they do not respond at first.**

Here are more suggestions for using a witnessing booklet.

- As you read the booklet, be sure to allow time and provide an opportunity for the person to pray to receive Christ.
- Be sure that you have left the individual with enough information, whether or not the person has accepted Christ. Phrase this part of your conversation this way: "Here are some things you will need to know when you are ready to receive Christ."

Read Psalm 119:153-160 during your quiet time today. Let God speak to you through this passage. Then complete the Daily Master Communication Guide in the margin.

HAS THIS WEEK MADE A DIFFERENCE?

Review "My Walk with the Master This Week" at the beginning of this week's material. Mark the activities you have finished by drawing vertical lines in the diamonds beside them. Finish any incomplete activities. Think about what you will say during your group session about your work on these activities.

As you conclude your study of "Look to Jesus," I hope you realize that by determining your life purpose and life goals, you have an additional arsenal of weapons to use in Satan's relentless attack. By following Jesus' purpose for your life, you can stay on course in your walk as His disciple.

---

1. These categories are adapted from *Continuing Witness Training* (Alpharetta, GA: The North American Mission Board of the Southern Baptist Convention). Used by permission.

WEEK 6

Stand Victorious

This Week's Goal

You will be able to stand victorious in spiritual warfare.

My Walk with the Master This Week

You will complete the following activities to develop the six biblical disciplines. When you have completed each activity, draw a vertical line in the diamond beside it.

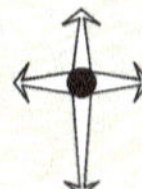

SPEND TIME WITH THE MASTER

◇ Have a quiet time each day. Check each day you have a quiet time: ❑ Sunday ❑ Monday ❑ Tuesday ❑ Wednesday ❑ Thursday ❑ Friday ❑ Saturday

LIVE IN THE WORD

◇ Read your Bible every day. Write what God says to you and what you say to God.

◇ Memorize Ephesians 3:20-21.

◇ Review 1 John 4:4, 2 Timothy 3:16-17, Psalm 1:2-3, 1 John 5:14-15, and Ephesians 6:18.

PRAY IN FAITH

◇ Read "Guide to Extended Prayer."

◇ List what you should pray about during the Prayer Workshop.

◇ Pray with your prayer partner about sharing your testimony with a lost person.

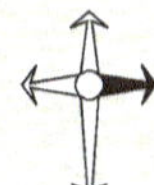

FELLOWSHIP WITH BELIEVERS

◇ Show God's love to someone every day this week.

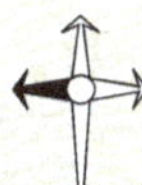

WITNESS TO THE WORLD

◇ Share with someone your personal testimony or a witness presentation.

MINISTER TO OTHERS

◇ Be a servant to someone who needs your help.

◇ Learn the Belt of Truth part of the Spiritual Armor.

◇ Explain the entire Spiritual Armor presentation to someone.

This Week's Scripture-Memory Verses

"Now to him who is able to do immeasurably more than all we ask or imagine, according to his power that is at work within us, to him be glory in the church and in Christ Jesus throughout all generations, forever and ever! Amen" (Eph. 3:20-21).

Now unto him that is able to do exceeding abundantly above all that we ask or think, according to the power that worketh in us. Unto him be glory in the church by christ Jesus throughout all ages, world without end Amen

DAY 1

Seeking God

Although you fight an unceasing battle against the enemy, you can conclude this study feeling confident that you have the ultimate weapons in prayer and in the Word to deliver you. The battle against Satan and against the forces of evil is fought first on your knees.

God has used many of my experiences as a pastor, an evangelist, a missionary, and a denominational leader to teach me this truth. One Scripture passage that has been particularly helpful in spiritual warfare is 2 Chronicles 20. This passage tells the story of Jehoshaphat, king of Judah, who was informed that a vast army of Moabites, Ammonites, and Meunites was on its way to make war against him. Read 2 Chronicles 20:1-4 in the margin.

"The Moabites and Ammonites with some of the Meunites came to make war on Jehoshaphat. Some men came and told Jehoshaphat, 'A vast army is coming against you from Edom, from the other side of the Sea. It is already in Hazazon Tamar' (that is, En Gedi). Alarmed, Jehoshaphat resolved to inquire of the Lord, and he proclaimed a fast for all Judah. The people of Judah came together to seek help from the Lord; indeed, they came from every town in Judah to seek him" (2 Chron. 20:1-4).

This passage sets the stage for the five principles of spiritual warfare you will study this week. Today you will focus on the first principle.

FIVE PRINCIPLES OF SPIRITUAL WARFARE

1. **The seeking-God principle**
2. The knowing-God principle
3. The depending-on-God principle
4. The believing-God principle
5. The worshiping-God principle

To whom did Jehoshaphat and the people of Judah turn for help when they realized that they were at war?

____

SEEK GOD

When you realize that you are at war, seek God, just as the people of Judah did when they realized that the three armies were coming their way. The seeking-God principle states that you always first seek God in a problem. He knows the enemy you are fighting, just as He knew the three kings who came against Jehoshaphat.

When you realize that you are at war, seek God.

What one word in 2 Chronicles 20:1-4 describes Jehoshaphat's reaction when he heard the news that he was under siege?

Alarmed

____

Who joined Jehoshaphat in calling on God for help?

the people of Judah

____

When he realized that he was at war, Jehoshaphat was alarmed. The people of Judah joined their king in sincere pursuit of God's leadership. The seeking-God principle includes the mandate to seek Him not just individually but corporately. If you have a personal problem or a problem that involves others, such as your family or church, pray as a group for an extended time.

A HEART FOR THE LORD

Jehoshaphat's heart was devoted to the ways of the Lord, as 2 Chronicles 17:3-6, in the margin, illustrates. Turning to God was not something he did only in an emergency. He had sought God earlier when he began his reign. When you fight spiritual battles, make sure that your heart is wholeheartedly for the Lord.

Not only had Jehoshaphat sought the Lord, but he had also sought to bring others closer to God. Read 2 Chronicles 17:7,9 in the margin.

Scripture also reports that Jehoshaphat had made a mistake early. Second Chronicles 18:3, in the margin, says that Jehoshaphat had aligned himself with the wrong people. By aligning himself with Ahab by marriage, he had tried to fight the battle with someone who was not of the same heart. You cannot solve a problem by consulting someone who does not have the same commitment to Christ you do.

As you studied in 2 Chronicles 20, Jehoshaphat later learned to call on the right person first. The same seeking-God principle appears throughout Scripture. You see the small boy David fighting Goliath and winning. You see the people of Israel, though weak and enslaved in Egypt, delivered by God. You see a little boy's lunch being used to feed five thousand people. Dependence on God is the crucial element.

This week's Scripture-memory verses, Ephesians 3:20-21, describe what happens when you depend on God: more than you can ever imagine. Turn to page 107 and read the verses aloud from one to three times to begin memorizing them.

TRUST GOD

I had seen God at work in scriptural examples, but I had never understood the principle of how to fight in spiritual warfare until I discovered it in Deuteronomy 20. How do you go to war when you are surrounded by the enemy? The answer lies in Deuteronomy 20, Moses' message to the children of Israel before they entered the promised land.

Read Deuteronomy 20:1-4, which begins in the margin and continues on the next page. When the Israelites stood in formation to enter a battle with a more strongly fortified enemy, what were they to do?

Call the Priest to encourage them to trust God.

"The Lord was with Jehoshaphat because in his early years he walked in the ways his father David had followed. He did not consult the Baals but sought the God of his father and followed his commands rather than the practices of Israel. The Lord established the kingdom under his control; and all Judah brought gifts to Jehoshaphat, so that he had great wealth and honor. His heart was devoted to the ways of the Lord" (2 Chron. 17:3-6).

"In the third year of his reign he sent his officials Ben-Hail, Obadiah, Zechariah, Nethanel and Micaiah to teach in the towns of Judah. They taught throughout Judah, taking with them the Book of the Law of the Lord; they went around to all the towns of Judah and taught the people" (2 Chron. 17:7,9).

"Ahab king of Israel asked Jehoshaphat king of Judah, 'Will you go with me against Ramoth Gildead?' Jehoshaphat replied, 'I am as you are; and my people as your people; we will join you at war' " (2 Chron. 18:3).

"When you go to war against your enemies and see horses and chariots and an army greater than yours, do not be afraid of them, because the Lord your God, who brought you up out of Egypt, will be with you. When you are about to go into battle, the priest

shall come forward and address the army. He shall say: 'Hear, O Israel, today you are going into battle against your enemies. Do not be fainthearted or afraid; do not be terrified or give way to panic before them. For the Lord your God is the one who goes with you to fight for you against your enemies to give you victory' " (Deut. 20:1-4).

"Do not judge, or you too will be judged. For in the same way you judge others, you will be judged, and with the measure you use, it will be measured to you. Why do you look at the speck of sawdust in your brother's eye and pay no attention to the plank in your own eye? How can you say to your brother, "Let me take the speck out of your eye," when all the time there is a plank in your own eye? You hypocrite, first take the plank out of your own eye, and then you will see clearly to remove the speck from your brother's eye" (Matt. 7:1-5).

"By the grace given me I say to every one of you: do not think of yourself more highly than you ought, but rather think of yourself with sober judgment, in accordance with the measure of faith God has given you" (Rom. 12:3).

"Do nothing out of selfish ambition or vain conceit, but in humility consider others better than yourselves" (Phil. 2:3).

The people were to call the priest, who would encourage them to trust in God. When you go into battle against the enemy, make sure that you are not afraid but trust God. Fear is faith in the enemy. If you believe that the enemy is stronger than you and your God, you will not win the battle.

No doubt you have found yourself in a spiritual battle during this study as you have attempted to demolish the spiritual strongholds Satan has established in you. Today you will examine another area of your life in which you will let the Holy Spirit build Christlike character.

DEMOLISHING PERSONAL SPIRITUAL STRONGHOLDS

In previous weeks you examined the strongholds of bitterness, speech, lust, religious ritual, and greed. Today look at the area of pride in your life and prayerfully consider how the Lord might be directing you to demolish this stronghold.

Read the verses in the margin that address the stronghold of pride. If we have true humility, we work on our own faults first instead of judging someone else. We keep our opinions of ourselves in check, and we put others first instead of ourselves.

After you have read the Scripture verses, describe the area of pride in your life that needs to be demolished, what you need to do to demolish it, and the spiritual weapon(s) to be used in demolishing it. Later this week you will record your progress. Here is an example.

Stronghold to be demolished: the idea that befriending someone in need is beneath me; fearing what my friends would think if they saw me associating with someone who has fewer advantages than I

What I need to do to demolish it: set aside my pride and concern about what others think of me; do what God leads me to do.

Spiritual weapon to be used: Belt of Truth—to remind me of what the Bible says about the pitfalls of pride and to see myself as I really am in God's sight instead of comparing myself to others

Now you try it.

Stronghold to be demolished:

The idea that people from other churches or denomination know less than I do.

What I need to do to demolish it:

Set aside pride and prejudice against others. Allow God to speak to me through others.

Spiritual weapon(s) to be used: Belt of truth - to remind myself of how God sees me and others and how he uses us.

Show God's love to someone every day this week.

Continue to prepare your personal prayer journal, which you will use in the Prayer Workshop that follows this study. Refer to pages 87–89 for items you need to include in your journal.

Read Psalm 119:161-168 during your quiet time today. Let God speak to you through this passage. Then complete the Daily Master Communication Guide in the margin.

DAY 2

Knowing God

Today you will continue studying principles of spiritual warfare. Read the second way to win spiritual battles, which appears below in bold type. Write the first principle, which you learned yesterday.

FIVE PRINCIPLES OF SPIRITUAL WARFARE
1. The seeking God principle
2. **The knowing-God principle**
3. The depending-on-God principle
4. The believing-God principle
5. The worshiping-God principle

You will begin your study today by examining the knowing-God principle. Because you know God, you can base your prayers on—
- His person;
- His promises;
- His purposes;
- His previous acts.

GOD'S PERSON

In the margin on page 112 read in 2 Chronicles 20:6 the way Jehoshaphat faced the threat of attack from the three mighty armies. Underline words Jehoshaphat used to depict God's power.

DAILY MASTER COMMUNICATION GUIDE

PSALM 119:161-168

What God said to me:

If you love my word, you will find peace and develop an un-offendable heart, where you will not be hit by every dart the enemy throws at you, but will be able to stand firm in my word and your identity as my child.

What I said to God:

Thank you God for your word and for your revelation. Please help me to love your word and to meditate on it daily so that I will be fully equipped when the enemy comes to attack my heart and the hearts of those around me.

"O Lord, God of our fathers, are you not the God who is in heaven? You rule over all the kingdoms of the nations. Power and might are in your hand, and no one can withstand you" (2 Chron. 20:6).

How great is this God to whom you pray? It will take all of eternity for you to know Him, but you can partially understand who He is as you read God's Word or look at the heavens He spoke into being.

The Hubble Spacecraft mapped the universe and determined that this world is much bigger than scientists originally thought. They claim that we have just seen light that started 15 billion light years ago. They once thought that the largest structure in all the universe was something called the Great Wall. It was 200 million light years across. But with this exploration they discovered that the largest structure is 10 billion light years across. That is 60 billion trillion miles.[1]

Do you know how God looks at the universe? Isaiah 40:12 says that He has—

measured the waters in the hollow of his hand,
or with the breadth of his hand marked off the heavens.

Somewhere in that universe is what scientists would call a third-rate solar system with a small star we call the sun, around which revolve some planets. We call one of these the world God so loved that He gave His only begotten Son to redeem (see John 3:16).

How do you feel when you realize that the God who created a universe of this magnitude cares about you when you pray in the midst of spiritual warfare?

- ❑ **I can't believe that He would care for me that much.**
- ☒ **I want to call on His power to defeat Satan in my battles.**
- ❑ **I have difficulty believing it. I feel unworthy.**
- ☒ **Other:** It makes me feel encourage that I am cared for by the creator.

GOD'S PROMISES

Because you know God, you can pray on the basis of His promises.

"O our God, did you not drive out the inhabitants of this land before your people Israel and give it forever to the descendants of Abraham your friend?" (2 Chron. 20:7).

Read 2 Chronicles 20:7 in the margin. On the basis of what promise does Jehoshaphat pray? God's prayer to Abraham

Jehoshaphat based his prayer on God's promise to Abraham in Genesis 12:3 to give the Israelites the land: "I will bless those who bless you, and whoever curses you I will curse; and all peoples on earth will be blessed through you" and on the basis of God's promise in Joshua 1:3: "I will give you every place where you set your foot, as I promised Moses." Jehoshaphat was saying, "We're in the land You promised us, and now these armies are trying to take it away from us."

In 2 Chronicles 20:8-9 Jehoshaphat cited a second promise.

"They have lived in [the land] and have built in it a sanctuary for your Name, saying 'If calamity comes upon us, whether the sword of judgment, or plague or famine, we will stand in your presence before this temple that bears your Name and will cry out to you in our distress, and you will hear us and save us'" (2 Chron. 20:8-9).

Read 2 Chronicles 20:8-9 in the margin. What did Jehoshaphat believe that God had promised He would do?

God promised to save the Israelites

When you are praying in spiritual warfare, base your prayer not only on who God is and what He does but also on what He has promised. Jehoshaphat believed that God had promised to save the Israelites. In many experiences I would have stepped back and not moved ahead except for the fact that God had directed me to act.

List the first two qualities of God on which you can base your prayers.

1. His Person ______________

2. His Promises ______________

3. His purposes

4. His previous acts

GOD'S PURPOSES

Because you know God, you can pray according to His purposes. Discover from the past what He wanted to happen. In 2 Chronicles 20:8-9 Jehoshaphat looked back at God's intention for the Israelites.

Read 2 Chronicles 20:8-9 in the margin. What was God's purpose for the people of Israel?

Establish them in the Land ______________________________

"They have lived in [the land] and have built in it a sanctuary for your Name, saying 'If calamity comes upon us, whether the sword of judgment, or plague or famine, we will stand in your presence before this temple that bears your Name and will cry out to you in our distress, and you will hear us and save us' " (2 Chron. 20:8-9).

Jehoshaphat reminded God that His purpose was to establish them in the land. He identified God's overall, long-range purpose, saying: "We're in the midst of Your purpose, O God. One reason we ask You to answer our prayer is that we're doing what You wanted us to do."

GOD'S PREVIOUS ACTS

Because you know God, you can base your prayer on His previous acts. Jehoshaphat did this in 2 Chronicles 20:10-11: "Here are men from Ammon, Moab and Mount Seir, whose territory you would not allow Israel to invade when they came from Egypt; so they turned away from them and did not destroy them. See how they are repaying us by coming to drive us out of the possession you gave us as an inheritance."

Jehoshaphat petitioned God on the basis of His past actions, saying: "They're coming up to destroy the land You promised us. If that was Your will then, how does this relate to Your will now?" This is what Henry Blackaby in *Experiencing God* calls a spiritual marker—a time when you knew that God spoke to you or led you.[2] When you are dealing with a problem in spiritual warfare, recall that time and ask, "God, how does this present situation relate to times when I know that You spoke to me or led me?" What God does is consistent. What He tells you to do now will be consistent with what He has told you to do at other key times in your life. His answer will continue the good work He has begun in you (see Phil. 1:6).

What God tells you to do now will be consistent with what He has told you to do at other key times in your life.

Daily Master Communication Guide

Psalm 119:169-176

What God said to me:

I will always be here to help you, guide you, and keep you. My promises are sure and I will never go back on my word. Continue to trust and believe that I always be there when you need me.

What I said to God:

thank you God for the reminder that you will always be there for me no what the situation. Thank you for reminding me that what you said or say will be, because you are God of truth and a God of your word.

Describe a spiritual marker that pointed to God's previous acts and helped you make a decision.

Moving to California (Dream I had)

Review the knowing-God principle by writing the four qualities of God on which you can base your prayers:

1. His person
2. His promises
3. His purposes
4. His previous Acts

Prayer is the cutting edge, the contact with God that makes everything happen. You pray on the basis of His person, His promises, His purposes, and His previous acts in applying the knowing-God principle.

Say aloud this week's Scripture-memory verses, Ephesians 3:20-21. Do you believe that promise? ☒ Yes ☐ No Repeat the verses several times to remind yourself of this promise. Review your previous Scripture-memory verses.

The ministry you provide someone might fulfill that person's prayer promise. Be a servant to someone who needs your help. You could help someone who is sick, homebound, lonely, or hungry. You can visit, write a card, or call—whatever you think would minister to this person.

PUTTING ON THE SPIRITUAL ARMOR

This week's study emphasizes the Belt of Truth, the last item in the Spiritual Armor. Turn to pages 129–31 and review the Spiritual Armor presentation, with special emphasis on the Belt of Truth. By the end of this study you will be able to explain the entire presentation in your own words.

Picture the Belt of Truth, which holds the rest of the armor in place. *Truth* means *integrity and moral uprightness.* Let it remind you to do the following.

1. Be true to yourself and to God when you pray or fight a spiritual battle.
2. Hold to the truth. Satan, the father of lies, would like to deceive you.
3. Master your emotions. Your emotions should be guided by truth rather than by the flesh or by Satan. The Bible speaks of the area of the body covered by the Belt of Truth as "bowels" (KJV), or inward parts, referring to the place where feelings reside or to the feelings themselves. The Belt of Truth helps you control your emotions and not compromise because of your feelings. If the Belt of Truth is not in place, you cannot expect your prayers to be answered.

Have you noticed that the Spiritual Armor covers the parts of your personality you studied in *MasterLife 2: The Disciple's Personality*? The Helmet of Salvation protects your mind. The Breastplate of Righteousness protects your heart, or will. The Belt of Truth protects your emotions.

Focus on the first of the three reminders. Stop and ask God to be true to you when you pray or fight a spiritual battle. Ask for strength not to compromise the truth because of your feelings when you are engaged in spiritual warfare.

Read Psalm 119:169-176 during your quiet time today. Then complete the Daily Master Communication Guide in the margin on page 114.

DAY 3

Depending on God

After you have sought God's help and have acknowledged His ability to deal with your problem, depend on Him to show you the way. Depending on God, in bold type below, is the third of five principles of spiritual warfare you are studying. Write the first two you have learned.

Depend on God to show you the way.

FIVE PRINCIPLES OF SPIRITUAL WARFARE
1. The Seeking God principle
2. The knowing God principle
3. **The depending-on-God principle**
4. The believing-God principle
5. The worshiping-God principle

WINNING THE BATTLE ON YOUR KNEES
As Jehoshaphat anticipated the siege from the three kings, the prophet Jahaziel arrived and gave him a word from the Lord.

Read 2 Chronicles 20:14-15 in the margin. Underline key words or phrases that gave Jehoshaphat courage in battle. Describe ways to apply these reminders when you are in spiritual warfare.

I can remind myself that no matter what I find myself in, God will always be there to protect me.

"The Spirit of the Lord came upon Jahaziel son of Zechariah, the son of Benaiah, the son of Jeiel, the son of Mattaniah, a Levite and a descendant of Asaph, as he stood in the assembly. He said, 'Listen, King Jehoshaphat and all who live in Judah and Jerusalem! This is what the Lord says to you: "Do not be afraid or discouraged because of this vast army. For the battle is not yours but God's."' " (2 Chron. 20:14-15).

As the prophet reminded Jehoshaphat, God is in charge even in a desperate situation when you base your prayers on Him and His revealed will. Although despairing at such times comes naturally, God can win the victory against all human odds. Remember that it is God's battle and that He goes to war through you. Therefore, you can turn over the battle to Him and let Him be the mighty warrior rather than rely on your own strength.

"Tomorrow march down against them. They will be climbing up by the Pass of Ziz, and you will find them at the end of the gorge in the Desert of Jeruel. You will not have to fight this battle. Take up your positions; stand firm and see the deliverance the Lord will give you, O Judah and Jerusalem. Do not be afraid; do not be discouraged. Go out to face them tomorrow, and the Lord will be with you" (2 Chron. 20:16-17).

The prophet then advised Jehoshaphat about the next day's events. Read 2 Chronicles 20:16-17 in the margin. The prophet told Jehoshaphat that he would not have to fight this battle. In the midst of your battle seek a Word from the Lord to show you what to do. Prayer leads you to God's Word and helps you apply it to your situation in faith. If God tells you to go, you go with dependence on Him. You must first win the battle on your knees. Once you know that it is His battle, you can go in confidence.

ARMED FOR BATTLE

John Piper notes that "the word for *fight* in 1 Timothy *(agonizethai,* from which we get the word *agonize)* is used repeatedly in describing the Christian life."[3] Jesus said, "Make every effort to enter through the narrow door; because many, I tell you, will try to enter and will not be able" (Luke 13:24). Paul compared the Christian life to a race: "Every athlete strives and uses self-control in all things. They do it to obtain a perishable crown, but we do it to obtain an imperishable one" (1 Cor. 9:25). Paul described running a race, fighting a boxing match, and striving against the forces of his own body. In 1 Corinthians 9:26-27 he wrote: "I do not run like a man running aimlessly; I do not fight like a man beating the air. No, I beat my body and make it my slave so that after I have preached to others, I myself will not be disqualified for the prize." He strove with all the energy God gave him, and he kept his body under subjection.

Check the words or traits that most characterize you, fitting you to win in spiritual warfare.

☐ **generous**	☒ **dependable**
☒ **good listener**	☒ **realistic**
☒ **tenacious**	☒ **optimistic**
☒ **loyal**	☒ **level-headed**
☒ **affectionate**	☒ **creative**

Recall this week's Scripture-memory verses, Ephesians 3:20-21. Why are you to give glory to the Father?

He is able to exceeding abundantly above all we ask or imagine.

The Father is due glory because He is able to do immeasurably more than all we ask or imagine. Even fighting the most insurmountable battles is no problem for Him because of His power.

PUTTING ON THE SPIRITUAL ARMOR

In day 2 you studied the importance of putting on the Belt of Truth as you continued to learn the Spiritual Armor presentation. You learned three steps for putting on the belt. Review them on page 114.

Focus on the second reminder. Stop and ask God to help you hold to the truth of His Word and not fall prey to the lies Satan wants you to believe.

Read 2 Chronicles 20:1-29, the passage you are studying about Jehoshaphat's response to the three attacking kings, during your quiet time today. Let God speak to you through this passage. Then complete the Daily Master Communication Guide in the margin.

DAY 4

Believing God

God wants us to live by faith, based on God's Word. After Jehoshaphat claimed the promise the prophet Jahaziel delivered, he bowed and worshiped the Lord. Read 2 Chronicles 20:18 in the margin on page 118.

When God gives you a Word, claim His promise and believe. Accept the promise that God will take care of you, even when the odds against you seem overwhelming. The believing-God principle, in bold type below, is the fourth of five principles for winning spiritual battles. Write the first three principles you have studied.

FIVE PRINCIPLES OF SPIRITUAL WARFARE

1. The Seeking God principle
2. The Knowing God principle
3. The Depending on God principle
4. **The believing-God principle**
5. The worshiping-God principle

SIGNS THAT YOU BELIEVE

One way to know that a person has believed God is when he or she begins praising God for what He has promised. Because he was aware of God's promise, Jehoshaphat praised God. He had reverence for God because of His mighty acts. Jehoshaphat knew who had spoken, and he believed. Before he took any other action, he bowed before God, who was worthy of his praise.

DAILY MASTER COMMUNICATION GUIDE

2 CHRONICLES 20:1-29

What God said to me:

Right now you feel like you're stuck and you don't know what to do. Do not rely on your human knowledge, but look to me to give you wisdom of what to do in or to get you where you need to be.

What I said to God:

Thank you God for the comfort of knowing that you will always be there when we need you. Help me to not lean to my own understanding, but to seek you and trust you, and know that you are still in charge.

"Jehoshaphat bowed with his face to the ground, and all the people of Judah and Jerusalem fell down in worship before the Lord" (2 Chron. 20:18).

Jehoshaphat demonstrated his faith not only when he praised God but also when he led others to praise. Read verse 19 in the margin.

The response of Jehoshaphat and the people is an important one for you to model. They immediately responded to the Lord's presence and work in their lives, based on what God had told them.

"Some Levites from the Kohathites and Korahites stood up and praised the Lord, the God of Israel, with very loud voice" (2 Chron. 20:19).

Follow Jehoshaphat's example by praying. If God has given you a scriptural promise for a problem, praise Him for who He is and for the way you believe that He will act.

"Early in the morning they left for the Desert of Tekoa. As they set out, Jehoshaphat stood and said, 'Listen to me, Judah and people of Jerusalem! Have faith in the Lord your God and you will be upheld; have faith in his prophets and you will be successful' " (2 Chron. 20:20).

The second way you know that Jehoshaphat believed God is that he obeyed Him. What you do after you believe God shows how much you believe Him. After Jehoshaphat and the people praised God, he acted on what God had told him. He believed and obeyed. Read 2 Chronicles 20:20 in the margin. Not only did Jehoshaphat believe, but he also encouraged the faith of others.

Early the next morning Jehoshaphat encouraged the troops and called on them to have faith. Even though he knew that the three kings' mighty armies were ready to overwhelm them, Jehoshaphat told the troops that they must march on. He believed, he obeyed, and he called the others to obedience. When you are in spiritual warfare, win the battle on your knees and obey the direction God gives you.

"An angel of the Lord said to Philip, 'Go south to the road—the desert road—that goes down from Jerusalem to Gaza.' So he started out, and on his way he met an Ethiopian eunuch, an important official in charge of all the treasury of Candace, queen of the Ethiopians. This man had gone to Jerusalem to worship, and on his way home was sitting in his chariot reading the book of Isaiah the prophet. The Spirit told Philip, 'Go to that chariot and stay near it.' Then Philip began with that very passage of Scripture and told him the good news about Jesus. As they traveled along the road, they came to some water and the eunuch said, 'Look, here is water. Why shouldn't I be baptized?' " (Acts 8:26-29,35-37).

The same principle of believing and obeying applied when Philip was told to go down to the desert and minister to the eunuch. God's directive probably made little sense to Philip. He had been proclaiming Christ in Samaria, where a great revival had occurred. Few people lived in the desert. But God knew that the eunuch was there, that he needed the gospel, and that he would then take the gospel to Ethiopia. This was all part of God's plan. Read in the margin the verses from Acts.

Identify a time when you obeyed God even though what He told you to do did not make sense.

____

God gives you the direction by which He plans to bring victory, but you must obey God to experience it. At times God calls you from the crowds—the big things—to one person, a seemingly small thing.

Continue memorizing this week's Scripture-memory verses. See if you can write them from memory on a sheet of paper.

PUTTING ON THE SPIRITUAL ARMOR

This week you have learned the importance of putting on the Belt of Truth as you continued learning the Spiritual Armor presentation. Review on page 114 the three steps for putting on the Belt of Truth.

Focus on the third reminder. Stop and ask God to help you master your emotions and to allow your spirit to be guided by truth rather than by the flesh or Satan. Ask Him to help you not to compromise the truth because of your feelings.

Explain the entire Spiritual Armor presentation to someone.

PRAYER WORKSHOP

As you approach the end of this study, you are preparing for the upcoming Prayer Workshop, when you will pray for a half day. Perhaps you wonder how you can pray for an extended period of time. Most people testify that after they get started, a half day is not long enough. In addition, most find the workshop to be life-changing.

To help you prepare for your Prayer Workshop and for future prayer times, read "Guide to Extended Prayer."

GUIDE TO EXTENDED PRAYER

Jesus Is Our Model

Jesus' entire life and ministry were bathed in prayer.
Jesus prayed on the following occasions.

1. When He was busy (see Mark 1:35)
2. When He was tired (see Matt. 14:23)
3. When He needed to make a decision (see Luke 6:12)
4. When He prepared to launch His ministry (see Luke 4:1-2)
5. When He faced the cross (see Matt. 26:39-44). When you face cross bearing or redemptive service, an extended time of prayer can prepare you for the trials you face.
6. When He felt the need—
   - for fellowship with the Father (see John 17);
   - for strength to perform His ministry (see Matt. 26:39-44);
   - to know the Father's will (see Matt. 26:39-44);
   - to intercede for others (see Luke 6:12; John 17).

When Should You Pray?

1. When you want to glorify God and express your love to Him
2. When you need fellowship with the Master
3. When you need guidance
4. When you need strength
5. When you face a critical or new phase of ministry
6. When you need spiritual awakening
7. When others need your prayers
8. When the Lord's will is not being done on earth
9. When laborers are needed for the harvest

DAILY MASTER COMMUNICATION GUIDE

ACTS 8

What God said to me:

My plans are perfect and you should be obedient to my word even when it doesn't make sense to you. understand that all things are working together for a good for those who love the Lord and are called according to my purpose.

What I said to God:

Thank you God for your perfect plans. I pray that I will always be obed-ient to your word, even when it doesn't make sense to me. Help me to always remember and believe that all things are working together for a good for those who love the Lord and are called according to His purpose.

Ask God to show you what you should pray about during the upcoming Prayer Workshop.

Read Acts 8, the complete story of Philip and the eunuch, during your quiet time today. Let God speak to you through this passage. Then complete the Daily Master Communication Guide in the margin on page 119.

DAY 5

Worshiping God

As the people praised God in 2 Chronicles 20:18-19, which you read yesterday, they had a great victory time before the battle. When you really believe God, you praise Him. And although they had not been to battle, Jehoshaphat was worshiping God. That brings you to the fifth principle of spiritual warfare, which appears in bold type below. Write the principles you have already studied.

FIVE PRINCIPLES OF SPIRITUAL WARFARE

1. the seeking god principle
2. The knowing-god principle
3. The depending on god principle
4. the believing-god principle
5. **The worshiping-God principle**

"After consulting the people, Jehoshaphat appointed men to sing to the Lord and to praise him for the splendor of his holiness as they went out at the head of the army, saying,
'Give thanks to the Lord,
for his love endures forever'"
(2 Chron. 20:21).

Jehoshaphat did something strange. Read 2 Chronicles 20:21, in the margin, to learn what it was. Why do you think he did that?

He believed god, that his people would not have to fight.

Jehoshaphat put the choir at the front of the army because he believed that his people would not have to fight this battle. He believed the promises he had received from God: "You will not have to fight this battle. Take up your positions; stand firm and see the deliverance the Lord will give you, O Judah and Jerusalem. Do not be afraid; do not be discouraged. Go out to face them tomorrow, and the Lord will be with you" (v. 17). God had told him that it was His battle, and Jehoshaphat believed.

"As they began to sing and praise, the Lord set ambushes against the men of Ammon and Moab and Mount Seir who were invading Judah, and they were defeated. The men of Ammon and Moab rose up against the men from Mount Seir to destroy and annihilate them. After they finished slaughtering the men from Seir, they helped to destroy one another. When the men of Judah came to the place that overlooks the desert and looked toward the vast army, they saw only dead bodies lying on the ground; no one had escaped" (2 Chron. 20:22-24).

GOD DELIVERS THE VICTORY

What happened next? Read 2 Chronicles 20:22-24 in the margin. At the very moment the people began to praise God, the enemy began killing one another. When Jehoshaphat and his people arrived, they expected to see a vast army but saw only dead bodies. God had been true to His word. They did not have to fight the battle after all.

This account from Jehoshaphat's life does not mean that you never have to fight battles. The secret is that the battle is won on your knees. The Lord fights for you. That is why David could kill Goliath, Gideon could defeat a host, and Samson could kill two thousand people by himself. Our problem is that we fight the battle on our own, with our own understanding and ability, instead of learning to hear and believe God. We must learn to obey, whether or not it seems to makes sense.

The secret is that the battle is won on your knees.

Describe a time when you tried to fight a battle on your own instead of leaning on God.

Working at St. Anna's and then quitting without having a job lined up.

When Jehoshaphat and his men arrived, it took three days to collect the plunder. Read 2 Chronicles 20:25-28 in the margin.

"Jehoshaphat and his men went to carry off their plunder, and they found among them a great amount of equipment and clothing and also articles of value—more than they could take away. There was so much plunder that it took three days to collect it. On the fourth day they assembled in the Valley of Beracah, where they praised the Lord. This is why it is called the Valley of Beracah to this day. Then, led by Jehoshaphat, all the men of Judah and Jerusalem returned joyfully to Jerusalem, for the Lord had given them cause to rejoice over their enemies. They entered Jerusalem and went to the temple of the Lord with harps and lutes and trumpets" (2 Chron. 20:25-28).

In 2 Chronicles 20:25-28 underline words or phrases that illustrate the fifth principle of spiritual warfare: worshiping God.

The battle of King Jehoshaphat against the mighty armies began and ended with the worship of God. You may have underlined "praised the Lord" and "went to the temple of the Lord with harps and lutes and trumpets." When you petition God, worshiping Him with thanksgiving in your heart is an important follow-up to that petition.

Stop and praise God for who He is. Thank Him for answering a recent petition.

Are you using the Praying in Faith form to pray about a problem, as you learned to do in week 4? Has God given you a Scripture that applies to your problem? I suggest that you apply the last three steps to pray in faith that He will answer. At the upcoming Prayer Workshop you will also review the six steps for praying in faith.

DEMOLISHING PERSONAL SPIRITUAL STRONGHOLDS

In day 1 you identified a stronghold you wanted to demolish in the area of pride. Today give a progress report on how you have used the spiritual weapon(s) you listed to demolish this stronghold.

How I am using a spiritual weapon(s) to help demolish the stronghold of pride:

____

Daily Master Communication Guide

1 Samuel 15

What God said to me:

Do as I command you without assuming what you think might please me or might make the situation better. When I ask you to do something, that is what needs to be done, nothing more nothing less.

What I said to God:

Thank you o God for your words of wisdom. Please help me to be obedient and do that which you ask of me without assuming anything or think that I know what needs to be done to make the situation better. Please let me not allow fear to make me disobedient.

RELATIONAL WITNESSING

Throughout this study you have recorded the names of lost persons on your Relational-Witnessing Chart and have focused on expanding your witness circle. You have learned how to use a witnessing booklet with a lost person. You learned in book 2 how to share your testimony with a lost person. Here is a witnessing opportunity I once had.

Having returned a rental car to a site about 10 minutes from the Albuquerque airport, I began talking to the driver who was taking me to catch my plane. He was a college student who was working during the summer to earn extra money for college. I asked him his major, and he told me. I asked him what he wanted to do in life, and he told me. I then asked, "After that, what?" He said, "I guess I want to get married, have children, make a lot of money, and enjoy myself." I kept asking, "After that, what?" until he realized that he had run out of time in this world. He said, "I guess I haven't thought about that." I told him: "It's really important for you to think about it, because only when you have answered that question do you know how to live. Only when you're ready to die are you ready to live. In fact, I was like you one time. I had an experience that changed my life. May I tell you about that?" He agreed, and I gave my testimony.

After I finished and we had arrived at the airport, I asked: "Are you willing to turn from your sins and confess your faith in Christ right now? We can bow our heads in prayer, and you can ask Christ to come into your life." He immediately did so.

Pray with your prayer partner, in person or by telephone, about sharing your testimony with a lost person.

Share with someone this week your personal testimony or a witness presentation.

Read 1 Samuel 15, the full passage about Saul's disobedience to God, during your quiet time today. Let God speak to you through this passage. Then complete the Daily Master Communication Guide in the margin.

On a sheet of paper write from memory the six Scripture-memory passages you have memorized during this study.

The Prayer Workshop that follows this week's work will be the finale of all of the prayer experiences you have had during this study. Use "Questions and Answers About the Prayer Workshop," which follows, to prepare for the workshop.

QUESTIONS AND ANSWERS ABOUT THE PRAYER WORKSHOP

Why Have It?

1. To have extended, uninterrupted fellowship with God
2. To evaluate what God has been doing and saying in your life
3. To solidify Christ's lordship in all aspects of your life
4. To receive guidance for future plans and ministries
5. To concentrate prayer on your major concerns
6. To intercede for others

Why a Half Day of Prayer?

1. It prepares you for a larger ministry. Jesus spent much time in prayer before He began another phase of ministry.
2. It is a basic building block in your continuing life as a disciple. You should have an extended time of prayer each month.

Extended prayer is a basic building block in your continuing life as a disciple.

What Should I Bring?

1. Bible (several versions and translations if desired)
2. The *MasterLife* books you have completed
3. Your personal prayer journal you began preparing in week 5
4. Paper or a notebook and a pencil or a pen
5. Life goals to date
6. Sack lunch, if your group leader asks you to bring one
7. Scripture-memory verses from books 1, 2, and 3

What Is the Schedule?

1. Announcements: 5 minutes
2. Individual prayer time: 3 hours
3. Share-and-prayer time for each member: 20 minutes
4. MasterBuilder presentation: 30 minutes
5. Wrap-up: 5 minutes

How Can I Pray for That Long?

1. Prayer is conversing with God. Listen to Him at least as much as you talk to Him.
2. Use as many or as few of the prayer resources in your personal prayer journal as you wish in any order. Include all of the elements of prayer, using "Guide to Thanksgiving" (p. 13), "Guide to Praise" (pp. 36–37), "Guide to Confession and Forgiveness" (pp. 54–55), "Guide to Praying in Faith" (pp. 67–80), "Guide to Intercession" (p. 100), and "Guide to Extended Prayer" (p. 119). You may also pray through the Disciple's Personality (pp. 127–28) and the Spiritual Armor (pp. 129–31).
3. Use your Prayer-Covenant List to pray for your needs and others' needs.

Listen to Him at least as much as you talk to Him.

Detect any patterns in what God has said to you and/or in what you have said to Him.

4. Use the Personal Guidance section of your prayer journal.
   - Read through your Daily Master Communication Guides to detect any patterns in what God has said to you and/or in what you have said to Him. Note the answers to your prayers, evidences of spiritual growth, helpful insights, and commitments or concerns you need to pray about.
   - Review your life purpose, life goals, and planning sheets. Ask God to help you write, refine, or complete these items today.
   - Focus your prayers on making progress toward your goals.
5. Read your Bible. Listen to God speak to you. Meditate on your Scripture-memory verses. Review your daily work in your MasterLife books and the applications you have made.
6. Do not become too introspective. Ask God to forgive your shortcomings; then move on to pray for other persons and concerns.
7. Think of your resources as a smorgasbord. Start with anything you want and return for more as many times as you like.

What Can I Do If I Think of Other Things?

1. Pray for whatever occurs to you. Perhaps God placed that thought in your mind so that you will deal with a certain issue.
2. Write down things you need to do later so that you can forget them now.
3. List things that continue to come to mind. Ask God why. You are not preparing a speech to give to God. You are communicating with Him mind to mind, heart to heart, and spirit to Spirit. You are dialoguing with Him even as you think.

How Can I Stay Alert and Awake?

1. Pray aloud.
2. Vary what you are doing, such as praising, reading God's Word, meditating, evaluating, praying for vision, and interceding.
3. Change your position often: sit, walk, stand, and kneel.
4. Get adequate sleep the night before.

How Can I Make My Prayer Time Meaningful?

1. Keep notes on what you do. Write down the time you begin and complete each activity.
2. Consult your notes in preparation for your next extended prayer time to ensure balance in your prayers. For example, if you spent most of this time praying about your needs, next time pray more for the needs of others.
3. During the share-and-prayer time tell the group what you did and how the experience affected you.

Consult your notes in preparation for your next extended prayer time to ensure balance in your prayers.

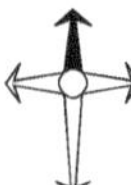

Write lists in your personal prayer journal of what you should pray about during the Prayer Workshop. Use "Questions and Answers About the Prayer Workshop" to prepare your lists.

HAS THIS WEEK MADE A DIFFERENCE?

Review "My Walk with the Master This Week" at the beginning of this week's material. Mark the activities you have finished by drawing vertical lines in the diamonds beside them. Finish any incomplete activities.

Congratulations on completing your study of *MasterLife 3: The Disciple's Victory.* I hope that you have learned how you can win the battle against the world, the flesh, and the devil by praying in faith and by claiming promises from God's Word.

Be sure to prepare for and attend the Prayer Workshop that follows this study. This time of fellowship with God may be unlike anything you have experienced before and will be an important step in your deepening relationship with Him. In addition, you will receive a preview of *MasterLife 4: The Disciple's Mission*, which I hope you are planning to study next. May God bless you as you grow in Christ.

The Prayer Workshop will be an important step in your deepening relationship with God.

1. Paul Hoversten, *USA Today,* 24 April 1992.
2. Henry T. Blackaby and Claude V. King, *Experiencing God: Knowing and Doing the Will of God* (Nashville: LifeWay Press, 1990), 103.
3. John Piper, *Let the Nations Be Glad! The Supremacy of God in Missions* (Grand Rapids, MI: Baker Books, 1993), 42.

The Disciple's Cross

The Disciple's Cross provides an instrument for visualizing and understanding your opportunities and responsibilities as a disciple of Christ. It depicts the six biblical disciplines of a balanced Christian life. *MasterLife 1: The Disciple's Cross* interprets the biblical meanings of the disciplines and illustrates in detail how to draw and present the Disciple's Cross.

Because *MasterLife 3: The Disciple's Victory* refers to elements of the Disciple's Cross and your weekly work includes assignments related to the six disciplines, a brief summary of the Disciple's Cross is provided here.

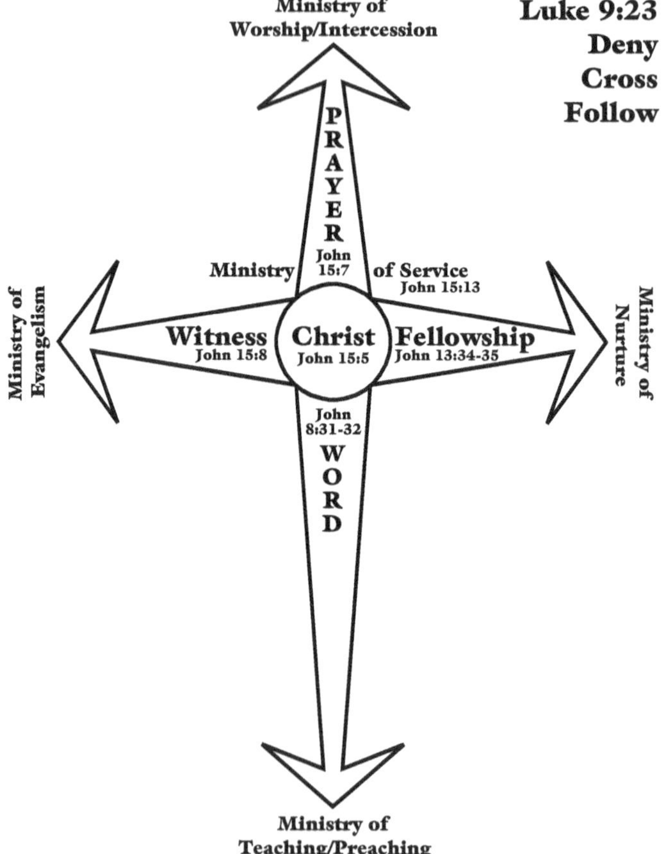

As a disciple of Jesus Christ, you have—

1 Lord as the first priority of your life;

2 relationships: a vertical relationship with God and horizontal relationships with others;

3 commitments: deny self, take up your cross daily, and follow Christ;

4 resources to center your life in Christ: the Word, prayer, fellowship, and witness;

5 ministries that grow from the four resources: teaching/preaching, worship/intercession, nurture, evangelism, and service;

6 disciplines of a disciple: spend time with the Master, live in the Word, pray in faith, fellowship with believers, witness to the world, and minister to others.

The Disciple's Personality

The Disciple's Personality provides an instrument for understanding why you think, feel, and act as you do and explains how to become more Christlike in character and behavior. *MasterLife 2: The Disciple's Personality* explains the biblical teachings about your personality and illustrates in detail how to draw and present the Disciple's Personality. Because *MasterLife 3: The Disciple's Victory* refers to elements of the Disciple's Personality, a brief summary of the presentation is provided here.

THE NATURAL PERSON

The circle in the center of this drawing represents you—your total personality. The Bible describes you as a unity. When you understand each element of your personality and how it functions, you will discover how to integrate your personality under the lordship of Christ. The Bible pictures you as a body, which makes it possible for you to participate in and communicate with creation and to be identified as a unique personality. The Bible pictures you as a soul, or total self, with the ability to think, will, and feel. The Bible pictures you as spirit, which gives you the capacity to fellowship and work with God. However, the flesh, or lower nature, entered our personalities at the fall of humanity. The flesh is the human capacity to sin and to follow Satan instead of God. The top door in the drawing—the door of the spirit—allows you to relate to God, while the bottom door—the door of the flesh—allows you to relate to Satan. Humanity's free will stands between these two doors. The big *I*—the ego—took over when the first human beings chose to turn from God and to follow Satan. At that point humanity closed the door of the spirit and shut God out. Consequently, people inherit a nature inclined toward sin and make deliberate choices to do things their own way instead of following Christ.

THE WORLDLY CHRISTIAN

The circle at the center of this drawing represents the worldly Christian. This person has opened the door of the spirit but has left open the door of the flesh. At some point this person was born again by the power of the Holy Spirit but failed to grow as he or she should (see 2 Pet. 1:3-11). The letter *s* in *spirit* has a capital *S* traced over it to show that the Holy Spirit is a part of

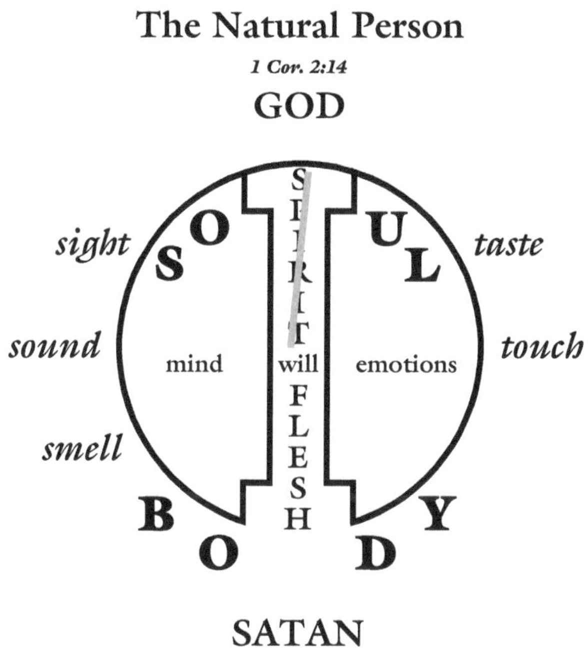

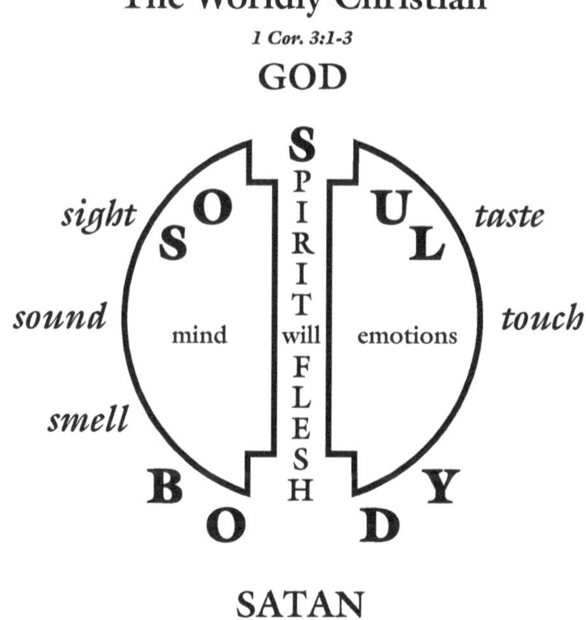

this person's spirit eternally. However, since the worldly Christian has the door of the flesh open in addition to the door of the Spirit, Satan still has access to this person. The world, the flesh, and the devil seek to dominate this person's thoughts, will, and emotions. This person experiences conflict and finds it is difficult to have victory in his or her Christian life.

THE SPIRITUAL CHRISTIAN

The circle in this drawing represents the spiritual Christian. When you open the door of the spirit, the Spirit of God enters your personality. As Christ's disciple, you are promised victory over the world, the flesh, and the devil. Your will is located between the door of the spirit and the door of the flesh. When you let Christ master your life, His death on the cross (notice the cross in the center of the circle) gives you a life of victory (see Gal. 2:20). Because considering your flesh crucified is an act of your will, Christ within you helps you keep the door of the spirit open and the door of the flesh closed. Because you are filled with the Spirit of God, God takes control of your mind, your will, your emotions, and therefore your soul and body.

HOW TO HAVE VICTORY

Here is how to make Christ the Master of your total personality:

1. Ask God to help you to will to do the right thing (see Phil. 2:13).
2. Open the door of the spirit to the Spirit of God by asking Him to fill you (see Eph. 5:18).
3. Close the door of the flesh to Satan by confessing your sins and by claiming Christ's crucifixion of the flesh (see Gal. 5:24).
4. Renew your mind by saturating it in the Word of God (see Rom. 12:2).
5. Allow the Holy Spirit to master your emotions by producing the fruit of the Spirit in you (see Gal. 5:22-23).
6. Present your body to Christ as an instrument of righteousness (see Rom. 6:12-13).
7. Love the Lord your God with all your heart, with all your soul, with all your mind, and with all your strength (see Mark 12:30).

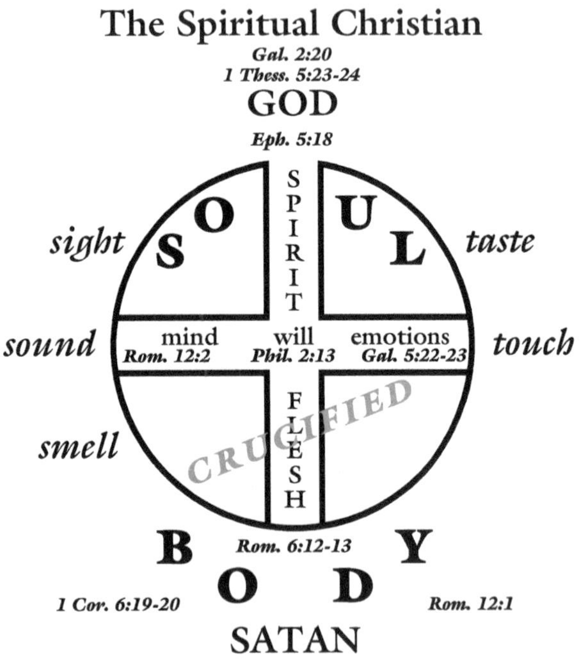

The Spiritual Christian

Gal. 2:20
1 Thess. 5:23-24
GOD
Eph. 5:18
S O U L
SPIRIT
sight
taste
sound
touch
smell
mind *Rom. 12:2*
will *Phil. 2:13*
emotions *Gal. 5:22-23*
FLESH
CRUCIFIED
Rom. 6:12-13
B O D Y
1 Cor. 6:19-20
Rom. 12:1
SATAN

The Spiritual Armor

Use the following presentation to explain to another person how God equips Christians to wage spiritual warfare. The material below is the presentation you make to the other person. Learn to present it in your own words in a natural way. Directions to you are in parentheses. You are not expected to quote all of the Scripture references. They are provided for optional study.

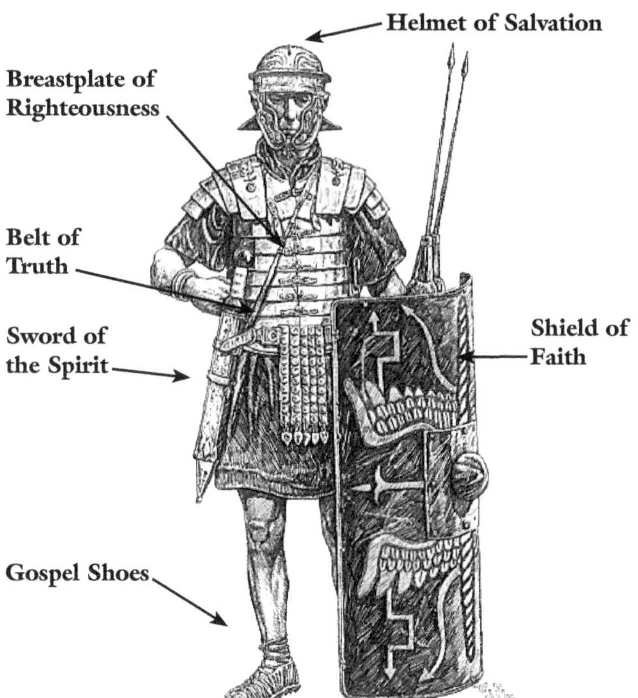

As a disciple, you know that you are at war. You have experienced spiritual conflict in your personality between the forces of good and the forces of evil. You have discovered that no matter how many battles you win, Satan always returns to fight another day. Remember that you are not fighting only a private war. You are a part of God's army, called to defeat Satan and his evil forces. You live behind enemy lines, and spiritual warfare continually takes place around you in the world.

God equips Christians to win the battle (read Eph. 6:10-20). He wants every believer to stand against Satan and all of his schemes in spiritual warfare (refer to v. 11). He wants you to stand your ground in the day of evil and then finally to conquer and to be standing when the battle is over (refer to v. 13). He warns that you are fighting not against flesh and blood but against rulers, authorities, and powers of this dark world and against the spiritual forces of evil in the heavenly realms (refer to v. 12). The way to gain victory over evil spiritual forces is to use the Spiritual Armor mentioned in this passage: truth, righteousness, the gospel of peace, faith, salvation, and the Word of God. Paul compared each of these spiritual resources to a part of a Roman soldier's armor. He knew each piece well because he was possibly chained to a Roman soldier.

It is significant that Paul concluded the list of Spiritual Armor with an exhortation to prayer: "praying in the Spirit on all occasions with all kinds of prayers and requests." A spiritual warrior begins on his or her knees. Through prayer this warrior clothes himself or herself with the other articles of Spiritual Armor before going out to meet the foe.

Verse 18 focuses on prayer as a specific arena of warfare, placing emphasis on—

- praying on all occasions;
- all kinds of prayer but specifically supplication;
- alertness;
- perseverance;
- all of the saints.

Spiritual battles begin with or should quickly move to prayer. It is one means God uses to strengthen you in the power of His might. When you have armed yourself with the Spiritual Armor, you can claim victories through prayer. Then you can move out to see these prayers answered in the battlefield of the world.

Winning the victory first in prayer is illustrated by an Old Testament account. Jehoshaphat was threatened with an attack by three kings (refer to 2 Chron. 20: 1-15). He called the whole nation to prayer. After the nation had observed a period of fasting and prayer, God assured the people in verses 15-17: "The battle is not yours, but God's. ... You will not have to fight this battle. Take up your positions; stand firm and see the deliverance the Lord will give you." The next morning

Jehoshaphat encouraged his people to believe God. He placed the choir in front of the army as it marched into battle. What an unusual attack force! What faith in God! By the time they reached the battlefield, God had caused the three enemy armies to annihilate one another. Israel walked out on the battlefield and simply gathered the spoils.

The secret of victory is this: first win the battle in prayer; then you can attack the enemy and claim the victory God has already won. Sometimes you must do more than march into battle, but you can be assured that God has already guaranteed you the victory.

You are clothed with protective Spiritual Armor. Your mind is protected by the Helmet of Salvation, your heart or will by the Breastplate of Righteousness, and your emotions by the Belt of Truth. As you march, you wear Gospel Shoes—the readiness that comes from the gospel of peace. In one hand you hold the Sword of the Spirit, which is the Word of God. In the other hand you hold the Shield of Faith. This armor may be used in at least three ways:

1. When you seek release from Satan's dominion in an area of your life
2. When Satan attacks you
3. When you attack Satan. You attack Satan when you enter his realm to claim, through intercession or witness, persons he has captured. First John 5:19 says, "We know that we are children of God, and that the whole world is under the control of the evil one." The lost and backslidden are under Satan's control, and he fights to keep them.

Let me explain how symbolically to put on each part of the Spiritual Armor through prayer.

THE HELMET OF SALVATION

Picture the Helmet of Salvation you received when Christ saved you. Let this symbol remind you to do the following.

1. Thank God that you are His child. First John 4:4 says, "The one who is in you is greater than the one who is in the world." Thank Him for your salvation.
2. Praise God for eternal life. The helmet protects you at all times in any battle. Praise Him for it.
3. Claim the mind of Christ. First Corinthians 2:16 says that we have the mind of Christ. It was given to you when you were saved.

Second Corinthians 10:3-5 says: "Though we live in the world, we do not wage war as the world does. The weapons we fight with are not the weapons of the world. On the contrary, they have divine power to demolish strongholds. We demolish arguments and every pretension that sets itself up against the knowledge of God, and we take captive every thought to make it obedient to Christ."

THE BREASTPLATE OF RIGHTEOUSNESS

Picture the Breastplate of Righteousness that Christ gave you and that has produced righteous living in you. Think of it as symbolically protecting your heart or your will. Let it remind you to do the following.

1. Ask God to search your heart to reveal any wicked ways in it (refer to Ps. 139:23-24).
2. Confess any sin (refer to 1 John 1:9).
3. Claim Christ's righteousness to cover your sins and to give you right standing with Him (refer to 2 Cor. 5:21). Keep the breastplate firmly fastened in place with upright character and righteous living.

   Psalm 66:18 says,

If I had cherished sin in my heart,
the Lord would not have listened.

THE BELT OF TRUTH

Picture the Belt of Truth, which holds the rest of the armor in place. *Truth* means *integrity* and *moral uprightness.* Let the Belt of Truth remind you to do the following.

1. Be true to yourself and to God when you pray or fight a spiritual battle.
2. Hold to the truth. Satan, the father of lies, would like to deceive you.
3. Master your emotions. Your emotions should be guided by truth rather than by the flesh or by Satan. The Bible speaks of the area of the body covered by the Belt of Truth as "bowels" (KJV), or inward parts, referring to the place where feelings reside or to the feelings themselves. The Belt of Truth helps you control your emotions and not compromise because of your feelings. If the Belt of Truth is not in place, you cannot expect your prayers to be answered.

James 4:3 says, "When you ask, you do not receive, because you ask with wrong motives, that you may spend what you get on your pleasures."

THE GOSPEL SHOES

Picture on your feet a soldier's studded sandals. The Gospel Shoes—the readiness that comes from the gospel of peace—means that you are prepared for battle. Let this gospel of peace remind you to do the following.

1. Be prepared. Get ready before the battle begins. Pray that God will prepare you for any possibility.
2. Share the gospel. The readiness that comes from the gospel of peace is being ready to proclaim the gospel. Ask God to prepare you to witness for Him.
3. Intercede for the lost. You are prepared to attack the enemy through prayer or through witness. Paul was effective in witness because he prayed for the lost (refer to Rom. 10:1). Pray for lost friends on your prayer lists. Visualize the countries of the world, with their millions of lost people, and pray for their salvation.

First Timothy 2:1,3-4 says: "I urge, then, first of all, that requests, prayers, intercession and thanksgiving be made for everyone. This is good, and pleases God our Savior, who wants all men to be saved and to come to a knowledge of the truth."

THE SHIELD OF FAITH

Above all, picture yourself holding the Shield of Faith in your left hand. The Roman shield was a long, oblong piece of wood. When the enemy's fiery arrows hit it, they buried themselves in the wood and were extinguished. So as the arrows of evil are aimed at you, advance with the Shield of Faith and quench the fiery darts of the wicked. Let the Shield of Faith remind you to do the following.

1. Claim the victory. Faith is the victory that overcomes the world (refer to 1 John 5:4).
2. Advance in faith. Faith without works is dead (refer to Jas. 2:20). Put feet to your prayers.
3. Quench all of the fiery darts of the wicked.

Mark 11:24 says, "I tell you, whatever you ask for in prayer, believe that you have received it, and it will be yours."

THE SWORD OF THE SPIRIT

Picture the Sword of the Spirit, the Word of God, in your right hand. *Word* here means *God's utterance,* referring to God's speaking to you about specific situations. Let the sword in your hand remind you to do the following.

1. Grasp the Word. According to Hebrews 4:12, God's Word is an offensive weapon and "is living and active. Sharper than any double-edge sword, it penetrates even to dividing soul and spirit, joints and marrow; it judges the thoughts and attitudes of the heart." Use it whether or not the enemy acknowledges that it is God's Word.
2. Let the Holy Spirit use the Word. It is His sword.
3. Pray on the basis of the Word. The Spirit will use the Word to reveal God's will to you and to help you know what to pray for (refer to John 16:13-15) and do.

Matthew 4:1-10 says that Jesus prayed and fasted for 40 days, but when Jesus was tempted, God's Word put Satan to flight.

PRAYER BATTLES

The Spiritual Armor prepares you to intercede for others. Now you are in a position to pray for others and to expect an answer. Ephesians 6:18 says: "Pray in the Spirit on all occasions with all kinds of prayers and requests. With this in mind, be alert and always keep on praying for all the saints." The battle is on! Advance dressed in the armor of God. Persevere in intercession until the victory is won and you stand victorious with your trophies of grace. Pray that God's plan will be executed and that His gospel will be proclaimed boldly (refer to Eph. 6:19-20).

This kind of prayer requires more than five minutes. It may take an hour, a day, a week, or longer. Every advance of the Kingdom depends on the prayers of the saints. God has made you a partner in establishing the Kingdom and commands you to put on the Spiritual Armor in prayer and then to enter spiritual warfare.

Set aside special times for prayer warfare in addition to regular times of prayer. Begin with an hour a week and expand the time to a day of fasting and prayer. God intends that every believer pray always "with all kinds of prayers and requests." When God wants to do something in the world, He moves people to pray for it. Our greatest privilege is to fight in His army on behalf of others.

The battle in prayer prepares you for the battle in the world. Without prayer you go into battle without the whole armor of God. Use the spiritual weapons as you move behind enemy lines.

God's Word in Your Heart and Hand

Use the following presentation to explain to others how to get God's Word into their hearts and lives. The material below is the presentation you make to others. Learn to present it in your own words in a natural way. Directions to you are in parentheses.

As you pray through the Spiritual Armor, imagine yourself grasping the Word of God in your hand as you hold the Sword of the Spirit. The following illustration will show you how to grasp God's Word in your hand so that no one can take it away. The illustration is divided into three levels so that you can choose the levels appropriate for a specific situation.

LEVEL 1: DEMONSTRATION

Hear the Word. You can use your hand to illustrate how to live in the Word and to get the Word into your heart. Your little finger illustrates the first way you receive the Word. (Point to your little finger.)

Can you tell me the simplest way to receive the Word—a way almost anyone can receive it? (Allow time for the person to respond. Affirm responses that convey the idea of hearing.)

Hearing the Word is the first way you receive it. Even a child or a person who cannot read can hear the Word.

Think about the Word. The second way you live in the Word and the Word lives in you is to think about it

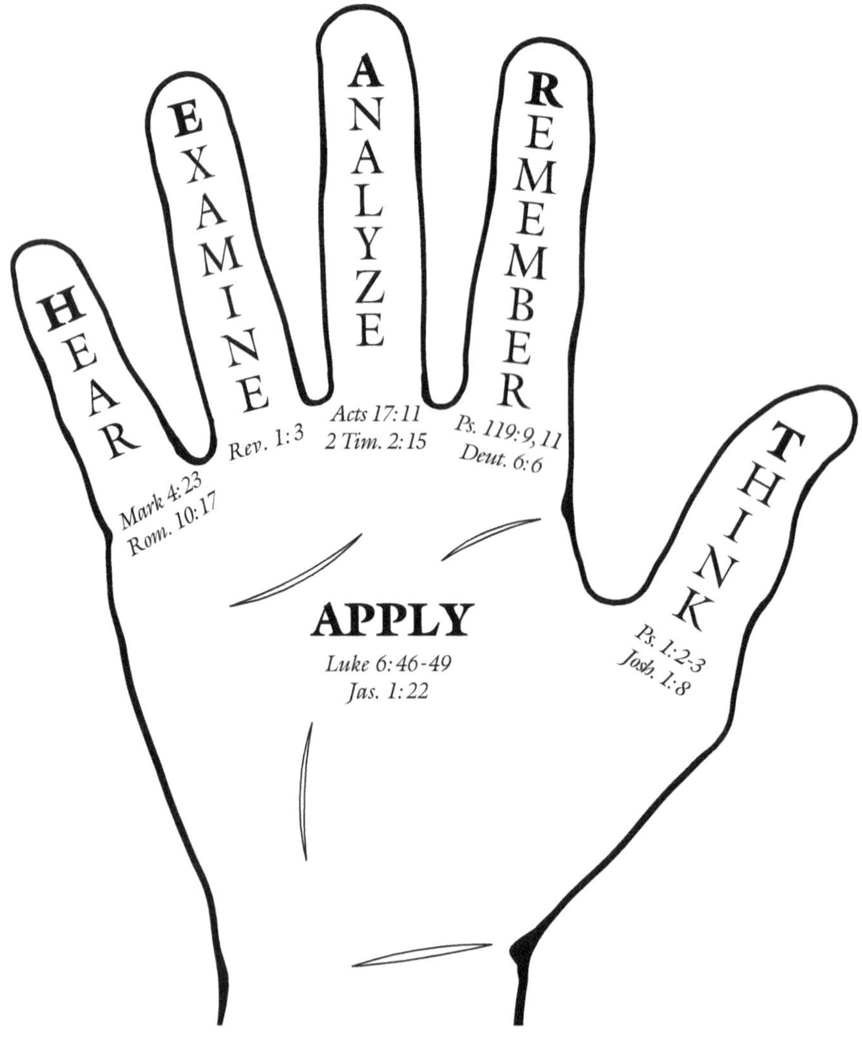

or meditate on it. The thumb represents this function. (Point to your thumb.)

When I grip a Bible with my little finger—which is "hear"—and my thumb—which is "think about what I hear" (for example, the pastor's sermon)—then I have a grasp of God's Word. But I do not have a firm enough grasp to hold it if someone else tries to take it from me.

(Tell the person to take the Bible from you while you grip it with your finger and thumb.) See, I can't grasp it firmly.

Examine the Word. Therefore, the ring finger becomes important. (Point to your ring finger.) This finger represents the next way you understand God's Word. What is that? (Allow time for the person to respond. Affirm responses that convey the idea of examining.)

Yes, examining, or reading, the Word is an additional way to abide in the Word; it helps you go deeper. But even with this level added, someone can still take the Bible out of my hand if he or she wants to.

(Tell the person to pull the Bible from your grasp while you hold it with the two fingers and the thumb.)

Analyze the Word. What is a way to live more deeply in the Word and to get it into your heart? (Allow time for the person to respond. Affirm responses that convey the idea of analyzing.)

When you analyze, or study, the Word, you go deeper into it. The middle finger represents analyzing the Word. (Point to your middle finger.)

When I hear, think about, examine, and analyze the Word, someone has more difficulty taking it from my grasp. Can you still take it from me? (Holding the Bible with the three fingers and the thumb, allow the person to pull it from your grasp after a struggle.)

Remember the Word. The most effective way to get the Word into your heart is illustrated by the index finger. (Point to your index finger.) Which way is that? (Allow time for the person to respond. Affirm responses that convey the idea of remembering.)

When you remember, or memorize, the Word, it really lives in you, you live in it, and God's promises become your possessions. If I hear, think about, examine, analyze, and remember the Word, I have a firm grasp of it, and no one can take it from me. (Grasping the Bible by the spine, tell the person to try to take it from your grasp, but pull it out of his or her grasp.)

Apply the Word. Another way to get a firm grasp on God's Word is to apply it. Notice that I held the Bible so that it fit firmly in the palm of my hand. Getting the Word into your heart is essential, but the only way to abide fully in the Word is to apply it to your life.

LEVEL 2: EXPLANATION

Now I will add Scripture references to the points in the hand presentation. (Place your right hand palm up or left hand palm down on a sheet of paper and draw an outline around it like the one shown on p. 132.)

(Write *Hear* on the little finger with a capital *H* at the tip of the finger. As you quote or read the verse, write the reference *Mark 4:23.*) "If anyone has ears to hear, let him hear." (As you quote or read the verse, write the reference *Romans 10:17.*) "Faith comes from hearing the message, and the message is heard through the word of Christ."

(Write *Think* on the thumb with a capital *T* at the tip of the thumb. As you quote or read the verses, write the reference *Psalm 1:2-3.*)

His delight is in the law of the Lord,
and on his law he meditates day and night.

(As you quote or read the verse, write the reference *Joshua 1:8.*) "Do not let this Book of the Law depart from your mouth; meditate on it day and night, so that you may be careful to do everything written in it. Then you will be prosperous and successful."

(Write *Examine* on the ring finger with a capital *E* at the tip of the finger. As you quote or read the verse, write the reference *Revelation 1:3.*) "Blessed is the one who reads the words of this prophecy, and blessed are those who hear it and take to heart what is written in it, because the time is near."

(Write *Analyze* on the middle finger with a capital *A* at the tip of the finger. As you quote or read the verse, write the reference *Acts 17:11.*) "The Bereans were of more noble character than the Thessalonians, for they received the message with great eagerness and examined the Scriptures every day to see if what Paul said was true." (As you quote or read the verse, write the reference *2 Timothy 2:15.*) "Do your best to present yourself to God as one approved, a workman who does not need to be ashamed and who correctly handles the word of truth."

(Write *Remember* on the index finger with a capital *R* at the tip of the finger. As you quote or read the verses, write the reference *Psalm 119:9,11.*)

How can a young man keep his way pure?
By living according to your word.
I have hidden your word in my heart
that I might not sin against you.

(As you quote or read the verse, write the reference *Deuteronomy 6:6.*) "These commandments that I give you today are to be upon your hearts."

(In the center of the hand write *Apply.* As you quote or read the verses, write the reference *Luke 6:46-49.*) " 'Why do you call me, "Lord, Lord," and do not do what I say? I will show you what he is like who comes to me and hears my words and puts them into practice. He is like a man building a house, who dug down deep and laid the foundation on rock. When a flood came, the torrent struck that house but could not shake it, because it was well built. But the one who hears my words and does not put them into practice is like a man who built a house on the ground without a foundation. The moment the torrent struck that house, it collapsed and its destruction was complete." What was the difference between the two men who built the house? Both of them heard, but only one acted. (As you quote or read the verse, write a second reference, *James 1:22.*) "Do not merely listen to the word, and so deceive yourselves. Do what it says."

Look at the letters written at the tips of the three middle fingers. What do you see? (*ear*) Now add the little finger, and you have what Jesus said to do with your ears. (*hear*)

Now read the letters at the tips of all five fingers. What word do they spell? (*heart*) That is the way to get God's Word into your heart. And the word *apply* in the center of the hand is the way to get His Word into your life.

LEVEL 3: ILLUSTRATION

Let me explain why having a good grasp of the Word is so important. The Bible uses several illustrations for itself. As I mention each symbol and its Scripture reference, tell me why a firm grasp of the Word is necessary for effective application.

One symbol for the Word is found in Jeremiah 15:16—

When your words came, I ate them;
they were my joy and my heart's delight,
for I bear your name,
O Lord God Almighty

—and in Matthew 4:4: "Jesus answered, 'It is written: "Man does not live on bread alone, but on every word that comes from the mouth of God." ' " In these passages the Word is pictured as food. How would a good grasp of the Word allow you to use it as food? (The person's response should convey the idea of drawing nourishment from it and nourishing others, satisfying your own spiritual hunger and the spiritual hunger of others.)

Another symbol is light, found in Psalm 119:105:

Your word is a lamp to my feet
and a light for my path.

How would a grasp of the lamp of the Word help you apply it? (The person's response should convey the idea of being able to hold the lamp so that you could see, being able to take it with you, being able to light another lamp, and so on.)

Other symbols in the Bible include fire and a hammer in Jeremiah 23:29: " 'Is not my word like fire,' " declares the Lord, " 'and like a hammer that breaks a rock in pieces?' " Imagine trying to use either a hammer or fire if you did not have a good grasp of it.

Perhaps the most important symbol for the Word is the sword. Ephesians 6:17 says, "Take the helmet of salvation and the sword of the Spirit, which is the word of God." Imagine how dangerous it would be to wield such a sharp and powerful weapon without having a good grasp of it.

The more you get God's Word into your heart, the better you can use it and apply it. This simple illustration shows you how you can abide in the Word.

Relational-Witnessing Chart

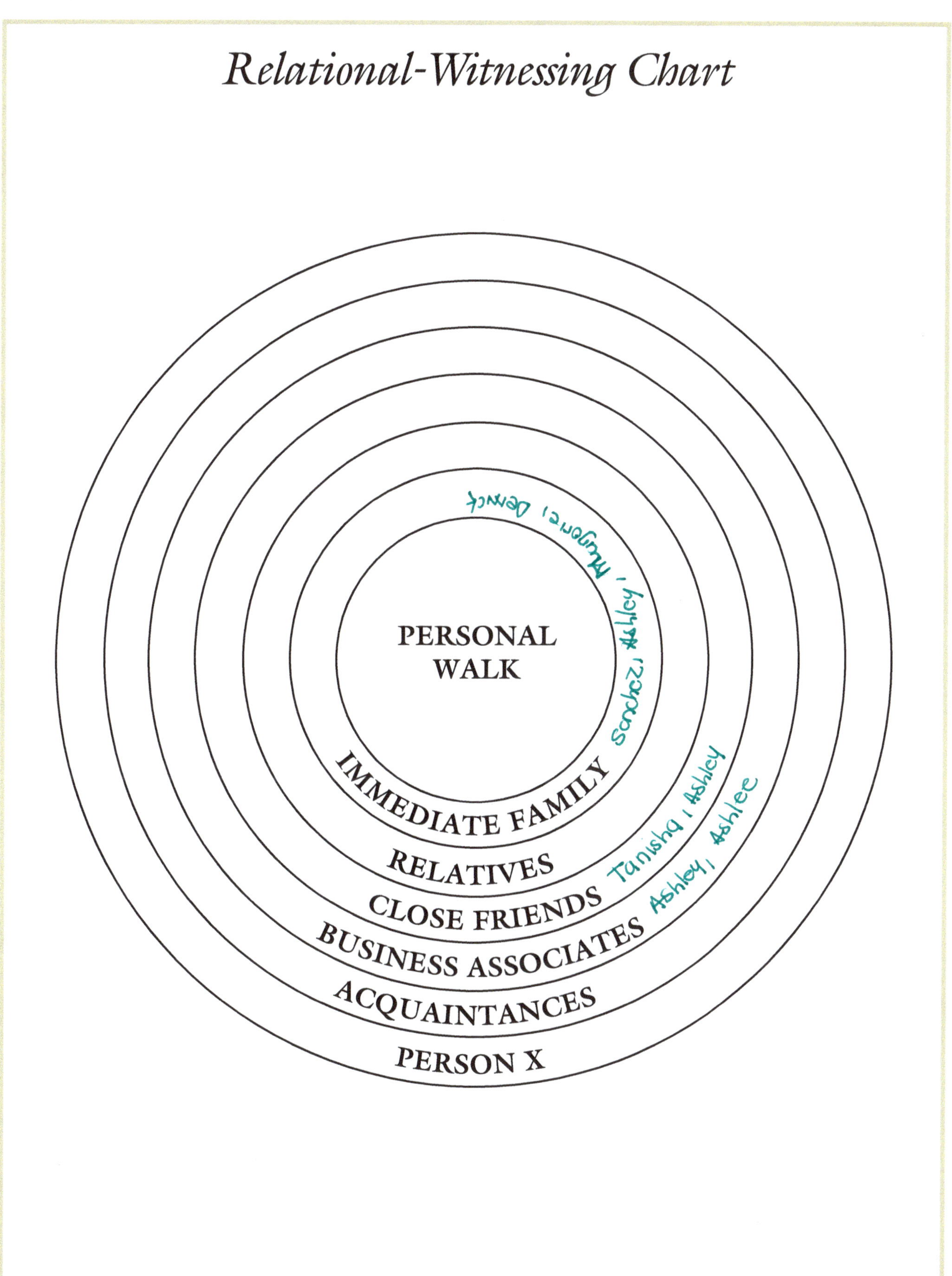

Guide to Meditation

Date ______________________________

Verse reference ______________________________

Pray for wisdom and surrender to the Holy Spirit so that He will make the Word come alive in your heart.

Perimeter of the Verse
Read the verses before and after the verse to establish the theme and the setting, which will aid you in interpretation. Then write a summary of the passage.

____

____

____

____

____

Paraphrase the Verse
Write the verse in your own words. Say your paraphrase aloud.

____

____

____

____

Pulverize the Verse

1. Emphasize a different word in the verse as you read or repeat it.
2. Write at least two important words from those you have emphasized in the verse.

______________ ______________

3. Ask these questions about the two words to relate the Scripture to your needs:

What? ______________________________

Why? ____

When? ____

Where? ____

Who? ____

How? ____

Personalize the Verse

Let the Holy Spirit apply the verse to a need, a challenge, an opportunity, or a failure in your life. What will you *do* about this verse as it relates to your life? Be specific.

____

____

____

____

____

____

Pray the Verse Back to God

Pray the verse back to God, making it personal. Vocalize or write the verse as you pray it back to God.

____

____

____

____

____

____

____

____

Parallel Passages

Refer to other passages that emphasize the truth of the verse.

Reference	Summary Thought
____________________________	____________________________
____________________________	____________________________
____________________________	____________________________
____________________________	____________________________

Problems in the Verse

List thoughts or ideas you might not understand or might have difficulty applying in your life. Discuss them with a Sunday School teacher or with a Christian friend.

____

____

____

____

____

Possibilities for Helping Others Through the Verse

Write a way you can use the verse to help another person.

____

____

Protracted Study

Record plans for further study of this verse. List notes, ideas, and outlines.

____

____

____

____

Praying in Faith

GOD COMMUNICATES TRUTH TO ME

Step 1: Abide in Christ
What is the problem?

____

____

How could God possibly use my problem?
❑ A platform for God to demonstrate His power
❑ A blessing from God for which I have not asked
❑ An opportunity for God to develop in me faith, love, patience, or another Christlike character trait
❑ An opportunity for me to develop a more effective prayer life

Rewrite the problem in the form of a question to God.

____

____

Am I abiding in Christ and committed to His will for my life? ❑ Yes ❑ No

Step 2: Abide in the Word
Ask yourself:
- Have I brought my problem to God first? ❑ Yes ❑ No
- Am I systematically abiding in His Word? ❑ Yes ❑ No
- Am I willing to wait for His solution? ❑ Yes ❑ No

Step 3: Allow the Holy Spirit to Lead You in Truth
Am I allowing the Holy Spirit to fill me, to lead me to a Scripture, and to apply it to my problem? ❑ Yes ❑ No What is the Scripture? ____________________
How do I think this Scripture applies to my problem?

____

____

____

____

I COMMUNICATE FAITH TO GOD

Step 4: Ask According to God's Will
What is my specific request?

____

____

Step 5: Accept God's Will in Faith
What do I believe that God will do about my problem?

____

____

Do I accept God's promise as a God-revealed certainty? ❑ Yes ❑ No

Step 6: Act on the Basis of God's Word to You
What actions(s) will I take, based on this Word from God?

____

____

____

What action(s) did God take in answer to my prayer of faith?

____

____

What else do I need to do?

____

____

Date submitted to God ______________________________

Date answered ______________________________

Hearing the Word

Date ____________________ **Place** ____________________

Speaker ____________________ **Text** ____________________

Title ____________________

Message

Points, explanation, illustrations, application:

Summary
The main thing the speaker wants me to do, be, and/or feel as a result of this message:

____

____

____

____

Application to My Life
What did God say to me through this message?

____

____

____

How does my life measure up to this word?

____

____

____

What action(s) will I take to bring my life in line with this word?

____

____

____

____

What truth do I need to study further?

____

____

Weekly-Goals Chart

Date	Take Notes on One Sermon	Read Word 10 Minutes a Day	Study Word One Time a Week	Memorize One or Two Verses a Week	Review 12 Verses a Day	Pray 10 Minutes a Day	Witness One Time a Week	Exercise Three Times a Week

Prayer-Covenant List

Request	Date	Bible Promise	Answer	Date